CHILDREN, FAMILIES AND SOCIAL EXCLUSION

New approaches to prevention

Kate Morris, Marian Barnes and Paul Mason

This edition published in Great Britain in 2009 by

The Policy Press
University of Bristol
Fourth Floor
Beacon House
Queen's Road
Bristol BS8 1QU
UK

Tel +44 (0)117 331 4054
Fax +44 (0)117 331 4093
e-mail tpp-info@bristol.ac.uk
www.policypress.org.uk

North American office:
The Policy Press
c/o International Specialized Books Services
920 NE 58th Avenue, Suite 300
Portland, OR 97213-3786, USA
Tel +1 503 287 3093
Fax +1 503 280 8832
e-mail info@isbs.com

British Library Cataloguing in Publication Data
A catalogue record for this book is available from the British Library.

Library of Congress Cataloging-in-Publication Data
A catalog record for this book has been requested.

ISBN 978 1 86134 965 1 paperback
ISBN 978 1 86134 966 8 hardcover

Cover design by Qube Design Associates, Bristol
Printed and bound in Great Britain by The Charlesworth Group, Wakefield

Contents

Acknowledgements

This book draws on the work of the National Evaluation of the Children's Fund and we would like to thank all the colleagues who were part of this evaluation team, the staff who worked within the Children's Fund and the Department for Children, Schools and Families, and the children and families who worked with the evaluation.

We would also like to thank all our friends and families for their support and tolerance, including Claire and Bibi, Bill, Jenny and Daniel, and Dot Morris.

ONE

Introduction

This book seeks to explore the new understandings that are necessary for preventative policy and practice in child welfare in the changing UK policy context. The discussion and analysis draw on empirical data from the National Evaluation of the Children's Fund (NCF). But our aim here is not simply to report the results of that evaluation – we have done that elsewhere (Barnes et al, 2006a; Beirens et al, 2006; Edwards et al, 2006; Hughes and Fielding, 2006; Mason et al, 2006; Morris et al, 2006; Prior et al, 2006). In this book we are seeking to understand the Children's Fund in the context of changing ideas about child and family policy and broader thinking about the nature of social exclusion and how this might be challenged. One of the central concepts guiding the design of the Children's Fund was prevention (alongside partnership and participation). In very broad terms, the overarching objective was to stimulate and support the development of local collaborative services that aimed to reduce or prevent social exclusion of children and young people. But as we will see, the concept of prevention was applied rather more restrictively when it came to detailing specific sub-objectives for the Fund, and the slippery nature of the concept became very evident when practitioners started to consider just what types of activities focused on what groups of children would fit the criteria for 'prevention' set out in the national guidance for implementation. As a result of our studies of the way in which people interpreted and implemented the idea of prevention in practice, we suggest a way of thinking about what 'preventing social exclusion' can mean and the implications of this for different strategies that might be applied in different contexts.

As we explore in detail in Chapter Four, the Children's Fund was set up in 2000 as a catalyst to move forward inter-agency cooperation and child- and family-led preventative services in local authorities in England. It was seen as part of a long-term strategy aimed at addressing the risks of social exclusion and enabling children and young people to develop as healthy, responsible and engaged citizens. It was unusual in targeting children aged five to 13 – a group that had previously received little policy attention. It was more familiar in its appeal to 'partnership and participation' as key to enabling effective solutions to previous policy failures, and in its objective of contributing to the reduction of social exclusion. Thus, it can be seen as one of a raft of social policy initiatives launched by New Labour that were intended to produce more collaborative working and more cohesive families and communities.

Evaluating the Children's Fund

Like most of such policy initiatives, the establishment of the Children's Fund was accompanied by a requirement to evaluate its effectiveness. Each Children's Fund partnership was required to commission a local evaluation and, nationally, government invested over £5 million in order to understand how the Children's Fund worked out in practice and what impact it had. This book is based on one strand of that evaluation. It draws on work conducted at the University of Birmingham between 2001 and 2005, which involved case studies of the approaches being developed to work with groups of children who might be considered to be particularly marginalised, on other work that considered how decisions were made to target children and young people for specific attention within the overall strategy of the Fund and on evidence about the way in which children and their families who received services provided through the Fund experienced this and considered that it had affected their lives.

The case study work adopted a theory-of-change approach to evaluation. This involved working with stakeholders to articulate their objectives, the ways of working they were adopting to achieve these objectives and the rationales underpinning these approaches (Mason and Barnes, 2007). The resultant theory-of-change statements then provided the structure within which the implementation of activities and their impact were reviewed. Theory-of-change evaluation enables researchers and those involved in the programme to assess whether the short- and medium-term changes expected as a result of the activities put in place are being achieved. This can inform longer-term implementation plans as well as enable an assessment of likely long-term outcomes (that is, those only likely to be achieved in five to 10 years – or longer) when evaluation does not continue throughout this period. The data collected included:

- reviews of relevant documentation, including minutes of meetings, partnership plans, local evaluation reports and monitoring returns;
- semi-structured interviews with strategic stakeholders and service providers;
- interviews with children and their families;

- activity-based data collection with children, for example diaries, group sessions and workshops; and
- observational fieldwork.

In addition to enabling continuing assessment of progress towards objectives, the value of this approach to evaluation is that it makes explicit the assumptions on which change programmes are based and highlights the way in which stakeholders define the groups that they are targeting and the problems that they are addressing. Thus, as well as being able to report on what was done and what difference it made to the lives of the children and families making use of Children's Fund services, our analysis enabled us to consider how those responsible for implementing the Children's Fund interpreted what it was about, who it was aimed at and how 'success' might be understood. This, in turn, enabled us to develop our analysis of prevention: what it meant and how it was interpreted in practice by those seeking to use the opportunity provided by the Children's Fund to improve the lives of children targeted by the initiative.

The structure of the book

The structure of this book is intended to enable the reader to explore broader policy issues before addressing the more specific themes of prevention within child welfare and the learning that has emerged from national developments and evaluations. The chapters are set out as follows.

In Chapter Two we consider the contested nature of the concept of social exclusion. We go on to apply the framework of social exclusion that we adopted in the Children's Fund evaluation to understand evidence about the circumstances of the four groups of children and young people that are the main focus for our analysis: disabled children, children who are refugees or asylum seekers, Gypsy/Traveller children and children from black and minority ethnic backgrounds. We also consider broader evidence about the welfare and well-being of children in the UK. This provides the context within which Children's Fund partnerships were seeking to develop new ways of ensuring child well-being and inclusion.

The focus of Chapter Three is on the way in which thinking about child welfare has developed and how different concepts have come to shape the discourses within which specific policies are framed. In particular, we consider ideas of risk and protection, the emergence of 'parenting' as a particular focus for policy action and the enduring but shifting significance of ideas about 'family'.

Chapter Four applies the preceding analyses to a consideration of the specific preventative policies and policy initiatives through which New Labour governments have sought to address the needs of young children and their families. This discussion reflects on the perceived failures of previous child welfare policies and highlights the main characteristics of recent policies that have sought to move away from an individual 'children in need' focus to a broad agenda concerned with the risks to children of social exclusion.

In Chapter Five we start to consider the Children's Fund itself. Returning to our analysis of social exclusion, we consider how Children's Fund partnerships sought to identify, define and target specific groups of children and young people that they considered most at risk of exclusion and thus priorities for action. We also discuss the nature of the strategies they sought to put in place to deliver preventative outcomes.

We consider what these strategies looked like in practice in Chapter Six. Here we describe the activities through which partnerships sought to achieve their objectives and what children and their families thought about them. We identify short- and medium-term impacts on children and their families, but raise questions about the longer-term effects of these initiatives and their capacity to address the multiple dimensions and processes through which social exclusion works.

In Chapter Seven we set out our thinking about different ways of understanding prevention, based on the previous analysis of the Children's Fund in practice, and relate this to the dynamics of social exclusion. We are able to arrive at a new categorisation of preventative activity, and from this undertake an analysis of the underlying assumptions about the relationship between children, families and the state that are contained within different ways of working.

Chapter Eight seeks to draw together the key themes emerging from the preceding chapters. Using these themes we are able to discuss our overall conclusions and set out the implications of developing fresh conceptual approaches to understanding the prevention of social exclusion. We argue that traditional approaches to prevention and preventative activity have struggled to grasp the complexity of the multilayered responses that are required. We go on to suggest that developing conceptual frameworks for prevention that recognise and utilise multiple dimensions of social exclusion is necessary to the development and support of effective strategies and practices.

TWO

Social exclusion, child welfare and well-being

Introduction

In this book we consider policies implemented by different New Labour governments that were intended to address the 'problem' of social exclusion among children and young people. In particular, we consider the experiences of the Children's Fund in this regard. So, what is 'social exclusion' and how does it affect children and young people? The adoption of a social exclusion perspective by New Labour in its early years of government reflected the aspirations for social change of a new government following long years of Conservative rule. Under the headline 'Social exclusion is about more than income poverty', the definition adopted by the government that shaped the work of the Social Exclusion Unit (SEU) was as follows:

> Social exclusion happens when people or places suffer from a series of problems such as unemployment, discrimination, poor skills, low incomes, poor housing, high crime, ill health and family breakdown. When such problems combine they can create a vicious cycle.
>
> Social exclusion can happen as a result of problems that face one person in their life. But it can also start from birth. Being born into poverty or to parents with low skills has a major influence on future life chances. (http://archive. cabinetoffice.gov.uk/seu/pageac0b.html)

The concept of social exclusion can thus be seen to encompass multiple factors that disadvantage children and the families into which they are born. But social exclusion has always been a highly contested term and some have argued that its adoption by New Labour as a basis from which to develop policy was never a progressive position. Here we consider key arguments about the nature of social exclusion and how it has been applied in practice. We suggest that it is important to understand the processes of exclusion rather than considering this as a 'status'. We then go on to consider evidence relating to the circumstances of children and young people and how different groups become excluded.

What is social exclusion?

Levitas (2005) has distinguished substantially different discourses of inclusion and exclusion that are evident within official policy and academic analysis. She characterises these as:

- a *redistributive discourse* (RED), which derives from critical social policy perspectives and highlights the necessity to overcome poverty and inequality if 'inclusion' is to be achieved;
- a *moral underclass discourse* (MUD), which locates the causes of exclusion in the moral and behavioural weakness of those who are excluded; and
- a *social inclusion discourse* (SID), which emphasises work as the route to social integration and cohesion.

The concept of social exclusion has been critiqued for diverting attention away from the material inequalities experienced by many living in poverty, suggesting that the poor are to blame for their own exclusion because of moral failings and offering a one-dimensional 'solution' in a new version of the Protestant work ethic. In the context of child and family policy, and in particular the emphasis given to 'parenting support' as a means of overcoming disadvantage, the discourse of social exclusion has been implicated in the promotion of parenting norms that reflect middle-class culture and identification of 'the excluded poor' as both victims and perpetrators of their own exclusion (Gillies, 2005, p 87).

The concept of social exclusion was evident in French social policy rather earlier than its adoption within the UK. An early definition indicates why European states were concerned about social exclusion. Politicians and policy makers were concerned not only about the life chances of those who become excluded, but also about the consequences of this in creating divided and fragmented societies:

> Social exclusion does not only mean insufficient income. It even goes beyond participation in working life; it is manifest in fields such as housing, education, health and access to services. It affects not only individuals who have suffered

serious set backs, but social groups, particularly in urban and rural areas, who are subject to discrimination, segregation or the weakening of traditional forms of social relations. More generally by highlighting the flaws in the social fabric, it suggests something more than social inequality and, concomitantly, carries with it the risk of a dual or fragmented society. (European Commission, 1993)

From this perspective, the objective of achieving the 'inclusion' of those who are segregated or discriminated against can be understood as seeking to ensure that individuals can 'fit in' and thus do not pose a risk to overall well-being. In particular, they are expected to take hold of every opportunity to ensure their employability, which will not only benefit themselves and their families, but also help to ensure social cohesion. This is the SID discourse identified by Levitas.

While critics such as Levitas highlighted the potential for social inclusion policies to impose normative expectations about behaviours, or to blame individuals for their own problems, the potential of the social exclusion analysis was recognised by groups, such as people with mental health problems, who experienced themselves as excluded, but whose circumstances had not adequately been understood by reference solely to material inequalities. While many of those people with mental health problems are poor, it is not only poverty that contributes to the experience of exclusion. A key strength of the concept is that it recognises the multidimensional nature of the experiences of those living in poverty and of others at the margins of society. For example, Berghman (1995, p 19) suggests that social exclusion should be understood in terms of the failure of one or more of the following systems:

- the democratic and legal system, which promotes civic integration;
- the labour market , which promotes economic integration;
- the welfare state system, which promotes what may be called social integration; and
- the family and community system, which promotes personal integration.

Lee and Murie (1999) suggest that at the core of the 'problem' of social exclusion is the lack of power of those who are excluded to participate as citizens, and it is this that resonated with many of those who feel themselves excluded from participating within the societies of which they are putative members (Barnes, 1997; Sayce, 2000). Identification of the multiple dimensions of social exclusion has led to the listing of groups who are, or are at risk of becoming, socially excluded. These have included single mothers, young people who have been in care, children in deprived households, disabled people unable to find employment, Travellers, refugees and asylum seekers and black people subject to racism (O'Connor and Lewis, 1999). Ward (2005) argues that the concept of social exclusion is also helpful in understanding the experience of lesbians, emphasising the significance of non-material as well as material dimensions of the experience of exclusion in this context.

Berghman's (1995) notion of systemic failures resulting in exclusions highlights the other major strength of the concept of social exclusion. When Townsend (1997) changed his mind about the value of a social exclusion perspective (he had previously argued that it diverted attention away from deprivation) it was because it highlighted the 'potential instruments' of exclusion. Veit-Wilson (1998) distinguishes between 'weak' and 'strong' versions of the concept by reference to the extent to which attention is given to the processes by which people become excluded:

> In the 'weak version' of this discourse, the solutions lie in altering these excluded people's handicapping characteristics and enhancing their integration into dominant society. 'Stronger' forms of this discourse also emphasise the role of those who are doing the excluding and therefore aim for solutions which reduce the powers of exclusion. (Veit-Wilson, 1998, p 45)

Social exclusion cannot be understood solely as an objective status; it is also necessary to understand it as a dynamic process, although once again this can lead to some rather different explanations. Byrne (1999, p 9) suggests that one characteristic of the MUD perspective is that it claims 'the poor do it to themselves' and thus they are implicated in the process of exclusion. But as Ward (2005) demonstrates in her study of lesbians' experiences of exclusion, processes of 'self-exclusion' (where these are appropriately described as such) are highly complex. Ward identifies the way in which lesbians' 'decisions' to exclude themselves not only reflected negative discourses of lesbian identity as abnormal or unacceptable, but also assessments of safety and risk, which were influenced by factors such as religion, cultural background and profession.

Others have taken different perspectives on the dynamics of social exclusion. Jordan (1996) argues that the processes of exclusion are economic ones and suggests that there is a need for a 'theory of groups' that explains how individuals come together in different forms of association to include some members for member benefits and consequently to exclude non-members from such benefits – conceived primarily in economic terms. Sibley's (1995) starting point is sociospatial relations. He suggests that we should ask questions about who places are for, whom they exclude and how prohibitions are maintained in practice. This includes legal practices and the practices of social control agencies, but also requires an account of 'barriers, prohibitions and constraints on activities from the point of view of the excluded' (Sibley, 1995, p v). Sibley makes links between sociospatial structuring and psychoanalytical theories of the self and explores the different spatial levels at which exclusion can be experienced: from the home to the nation state and beyond.

> If, for example, we consider the question of residential segregation, which is one of the most widely investigated issues in urban geography, it could be argued that the resistance to a different sort of person moving into a neighbourhood stems from feelings of anxiety, nervousness or fear. Who is felt to belong and not to belong contributes in an important way to the shaping of social space. It is often the case that this kind of hostility to others is articulated as a concern about property values but certain kinds of difference, as they are culturally constructed, trigger anxieties and a wish on the part of those who feel threatened to distance themselves from others. This may, of course, have economic consequences. (Sibley, 1995, p 3)

Analyses that emphasise the processual nature of social exclusion highlight the different processes that are implicated and thus the different dimensions of the experience of exclusion. We can suggest that these dimensions of exclusion include (at least) the following, which interact with each other in different ways to create multifaceted experiences of exclusion for different social groups:

- *material dimensions:* exclusion from material benefits such as sufficient income, appropriate housing and physical environments (Jordan, 1996; Townsend, 1997);
- *spatial exclusions:* restrictions on where people can live and on their mobility within and between places (Sibley, 1995);
- *access to goods and services:* this can include both public and private services. For example, people with mental health problems and those living with HIV can be excluded from financial services such as insurance, the design and criteria for access of welfare services can, in practice, exclude those in need of support and the nature of professional practices can sustain 'them' and 'us' discourses, which further contribute to the marginalisation of 'clients' or users (Batsleer and Humphries, 2000);
- *health and well-being:* poor health is a consequence of material deprivation, can contribute to increased poverty because of the costs associated with illness and in its own right can be a source of exclusion from social participation (Purdy and Banks, 1999);
- *cultural:* certain lifestyles are regarded as irresponsible, immoral or 'other'. Fear of the other can lead people to exclude those regarded as outsiders, whether that is a result of ethnicity, religion or psychiatric diagnosis (Fernando, 1991; Lewis, 1994; Sibley, 1995);
- *self-determination:* certain social groups, such as children, people with learning difficulties and those regarded as mentally incapacitated, can be considered incapable of (and in some cases legally excluded from) taking decisions about life choices;
- *public decision making:* in spite of the expansion of participatory practices in public decision making, assumptions about appropriate ways of taking part, the way in which participation forums are designed and negative experiences of lack of change resulting from participation result in exclusions from decision-making processes.

Understanding social exclusion as a process also opens up the possibility of considering ways in which it can be resisted and the locations in which resistance can occur. Power is exercised strategically at the macro level and in interpersonal relations at the micro level. Macro-level dynamics provide the social, political and economic bases of exclusion and set the context within which micro-level negotiations and renegotiations take place. At an intermediate level, social exclusion operates through social policies that allow differentiated access to services, through bureaucratic procedures and practices that regulate entitlements in accordance with set definitions, which may be exclusionary, and through professionals who act as gatekeepers to resources and decision-making structures.

At the micro level, the processes of interaction between service users and providers, and between people 'at risk' of marginalisation and those they encounter in their everyday lives, can either facilitate participation or act as barriers to it. It is at this level that service users and others who organise around shared experiences of exclusion or disadvantage often take the initiative through either individual or collective action in order to maximise their scope for manoeuvre and enlarge the range of options open to them. It is also at this level that they begin to challenge the way their social reality is constructed and resist forces of exclusion. In so doing they begin to impact on the situation and engage in redefining the problem(s) to be addressed, specifying their role within this process and developing alternative explanations and solutions to what is on offer.

Thus, Jordan (1998) highlights the strategies of people living in poverty who develop ways of improving the quality of their life by engaging in economic practices outside the mainstream. The disability movement developed the social model of disability to account for the marginalisation experienced by disabled people and used this to propose fundamentally different social policies designed to include rather than exclude disabled people from social participation (for example Priestley, 1999). From within black communities, one response to the impact of racism on black children's education has been to establish supplementary schools that question assumptions about cultural deficit within black and minority ethnic communities (Reay and Mirza, 1997). And Anne Power (2007) highlights the social capital that provides a resource for those living in low-income neighbourhoods, which enables children and their parents to survive in difficult circumstances. These resistances point to the way in which policies may be redesigned to generate more inclusionary outcomes that do not require an acceptance of dominant norms of behaviour or practice. They also highlight the significance of collective action among marginalised or excluded groups in challenging normative assumptions about the characteristic of 'the excluded'.

Child welfare and well-being in the UK

In 2007, the United Nations Children's Fund (UNICEF) published a report entitled *Child Poverty in Perspective* (UNICEF, 2007) that caused consternation in the UK. In spite of an espoused commitment on the part of New Labour to eradicate child poverty (see below), this report not only identified considerable remaining problems regarding children's material circumstances in the UK, but also painted a picture of unhappiness and poor relationships that suggested that children in many less affluent countries are happier than their UK peers. In this section we review evidence relating to the lives and circumstances of children in the UK in the early 21st century.

At the start of the millennium, New Labour set a policy objective of eradicating child poverty within 20 years. In order to assess progress towards meeting the 2020 target, the government set interim targets of a reduction of a quarter by 2004/05 and of a half by 2010. Despite a large reduction, of 600,000 fewer children in poverty, the first target was narrowly missed. While there was a reduction in the proportion of children spending a large number of years (three or four) in poverty – down from 17% in 1997-2000 to 13% in 2001-04 (DWP, 2006) – this still left 2.8 million children in relative poverty in 2004/05, and the most recent data at the time of writing indicated a *rise* of 100,000 children during 2005/06 (DWP, 2007a). Progress in reducing child poverty in the UK also needs to be considered in the context of the UK having had the worst rate in Europe at the time of the Prime Minister's pledge. Changes that have taken place since then merely bring the UK *close* to the European average. Indeed, in 1999, child poverty in the UK was higher than in nearly all other industrialised nations (DWP, 2007b). Children had replaced older people as the group most likely to be in poverty, as numbers doubled in the 20 years from the 1970s (Hirsch, 2007). The UNICEF (2007) report confirms the low placing of the UK in relation to child welfare in contrast to the European Union and to the industrialised, developed, world. Although criticised at the time of publication by the UK government as dependent on out-of-date data and ignoring the progress made since 1999 (BBC, 2007), the more recent data undermine this defence. While progress has been made, there is much to do to alleviate child poverty and its negative effects in the UK.

The UNICEF report made clear that child well-being cannot solely be equated with material advantage and that child poverty is evident in rich countries:

> The true measure of a nation's standing is how well it attends to its children – their health and safety, their material security, their education and socialization, and their sense of being loved, valued and included in the families and societies into which they are born. (UNICEF, 2007, p 1)

The authors of the report emphasise the necessity to address the multidimensional nature of children's experiences and both the objective and the subjective aspects of such experience in order to assess well-being. Tess Ridge's (2002) study of what poverty and social exclusion mean to children makes this clear. In order to understand what poverty means to children in their everyday lives, Ridge conducted interviews with disadvantaged children in both urban and rural areas. She explored how poverty affected children's capacity to *fit in* with their peers, to *join in social* activities and the particular importance of clothes as a key signifier of peer inclusion. All these were affected by poverty and constituted aspects of social exclusion that impacted negatively on well-being. Her work highlights the impact of poverty not only on children's abilities to access material goods that their peers take for granted, but also on young people's abilities to develop and maintain peer relationships. Poverty generates stigma as well as limiting experience: 'Missing out on shared occasions did not just mean shopping and leisure activities, but it also meant feeling excluded from the opportunity to meet up as a social group and to be included in group experiences' (Ridge, 2002, p 102).

Arguably, neither the moral underclass nor the social inclusion discourse prioritises children's subjective experiences of well-being in comparison to their performance as good citizens. But as the above quote suggests, a failure to encompass subjective feelings of inclusion or exclusion will provide only a partial measure of how well states are succeeding in fulfilling their responsibilities to their young citizens.

The UNICEF (2007) report summarises the dimensions of well-being and welfare for children. The dimensions that are measured are:

- material well-being;
- health and safety;
- educational well-being;
- family and peer relationships;
- behaviours and risks; and
- subjective well-being.

The authors of the report emphasise both the interrelationship between measures and the inadequacy of using economic poverty as the sole measure of well-being. Their summary across six indicators of child well-being placed the UK at the bottom of the 21 nations included in their study.

The UK comes 18th out of the 21 countries on the material well-being measure. This includes indicators for relative income poverty, workless households and 'reported deprivation'. Countries higher up the scale, for example the Czech Republic, have lower average incomes but a more equal distribution of income. The UK rates poorly for the measures of relative poverty and workless households, but settles around the midway point for the other measures.

Health and safety measures include infant mortality, low birthweights, immunisations and accidental deaths. On these measures the UK is placed 15th out of the 21 countries. The UK has a low placing for all these measures apart from accidental deaths, where it is placed second. Without this high placing, the UK would be in a far lower position overall.

The components of the educational well-being measure are achievement at age 15 in literacy and numeracy, as well as in science, the percentage of those aged 15-19 in education, the percentage of those aged 15-19 not in education, employment or training and the percentage of those aged 15 who expect to be in low-skilled work. The UK is below the Organisation for Economic Co-operation and Development (OECD) average and is placed 17th out of the 21 countries overall. While levels of basic skills are high (the UK is placed ninth), the UK scores poorly on other measures. The authors note that a lack of available data prohibits a consideration of early years education and of childcare provision.

The UK comes last in the measure of young people's family and peer relationships. The components of this are family structure, family relationships and peer relationships (the last two measures being derived from survey results). The UK has high numbers of lone-parent families (closely related to poverty; we return to this issue below) and although the rank for relationships with parents is 12th, the UK is ranked last for the percentage of 11- to 15-year-olds who find their peers 'kind and helpful' (again, we return to this issue below).

The UK is also ranked last for the measure of harmful and risky behaviours. This includes health behaviours such as healthy eating, risk behaviours such as drinking and smoking and experience of violence, fighting and bullying. The UK ranks low for health behaviours (17th) but last for risk behaviours, with a high incidence of smoking, drinking, drug taking and sexual activity. Only Portugal and Austria had higher numbers of young people who had experienced violence in the previous 12 months.

Surveys of children and young people's opinions were used to assess subjective well-being. Again, the UK is placed last on this measure, which includes children and young people's ratings of their own health, of their attitudes to school, and their self-reported life satisfaction and well-being. It is this final measure where the UK is placed again at the bottom of the OECD countries.

The UNICEF (2007) report does not directly address the issue of crime and its impact on the well-being of children and young people. However, crime does impact on young people and the reduction of crime was, as we will see, a sub-objective of the Children's Fund. Young people have increasingly been the subject of policy aiming to reduce crime and antisocial behaviour (Prior, 2005) but their increased likelihood of being victims of crime over other groups is less well recognised. The institutions and agencies of and around the criminal justice system have been shown to fail to address their needs as victims and witnesses (Mason et al, forthcoming). Crime itself is concentrated in particular areas and risk factors for involvement in crime include the area where a young person lives as well as factors related to poverty, with low income, poor housing and large family size all key indicators within the 'risk and protection' framework (Prior and Paris, 2005; see also Chapter Three). In the most recently available analysis of the British Crime Survey, young people (aged 10-15) were more than twice as likely to have been the victim of crime as those aged 26-65; the same analysis found that young people who had committed an offence were more likely to be victims themselves than other young people (Wood, 2005).

Another theme to emerge from Ridge's (2002) work is the impact of school and educational experiences on children and young people from poor backgrounds. Poverty can mean that children are unable to take part in school trips, and schools' demands in relation to uniforms, equipment and transport to out-of-hours activities effectively exclude disadvantaged children from important aspects of the educational experience. Other aspects of the educational system can also contribute to aspects of social exclusion. Ridge argues that the focus on education as a route to inclusion in adulthood has meant a focus on achievement within schools to the neglect of an understanding of education as a means of developing social, emotional and ethical skills. This narrow conceptualisation of education can itself be regarded as exclusionary, because it does not recognise the value of the different contributions that different pupils may make.

More recent research (Wikeley et al, 2007) has confirmed the impact of the lack of access to out-of-school activities for children from disadvantaged backgrounds. Based on interviews with 55 young people, comparing the experiences of those from families in poverty with their more affluent peers, the study highlights how poor young people participate in fewer organised out-of-school activities. The authors describe the benefits for young people who take part in such activities, including broader peer networks, self-confidence and skills, but centrally a different attitude to learning as a result of developing relationships outside of school. Young people from poor backgrounds are denied access to the learning that comes directly from such activities and also to the broader personal and interpersonal benefits they generate.

The relationship between educational success and longer-term life chances has long been recognised. In their review of the government's progress in reducing poverty and social exclusion, Palmer et al (2006) highlight the centrality of education to the eradication of future poverty, and the need to raise the level of attainment for those young people who are currently low educational achievers. They cite evidence that has only recently become publicly available, which shows that in 2005, 70% of deprived 16-year-olds failed to achieve five or more General Certificates of Education (GCSEs) at grade C or above, compared to 45% of those who are not deprived. Two thirds of those who fail to reach this standard at age 16 will fail to reach it by age 25. In his review of progress towards the eradication of child poverty in 2020, Hirsch (2006) argues that a focus on education is essential if the target is to be met as the current focus on work will not deliver the drastic changes required. In a separate publication, Hirsch (2007) reviews a recent programme of research (commissioned by the Joseph Rowntree Foundation: JRF) exploring the impact of poverty on education. The research, which includes the study of out-of-school activities and their impacts outlined above (Wikeley et al, 2007), demonstrates how low income is a strong predictor of low educational performance. The effects for poor children cannot be accounted for by school factors, that is, the quality of the school's teaching and resources. Whatever these are, poor children are more likely to do badly at school; those who do badly at school are more likely to be unemployed or in low-paid work, and thus be adults raising families in poverty. The evidence suggests that education policy targeted at raising standards fails to address the needs of disadvantaged children (Hirsch, 2007).

This analysis returns us to our starting point in this outline of child welfare in the UK. The government strategy to eradicate child poverty has had at its centre: work and the reduction of workless families and households. The strategy has four central dimensions:

- work for those who can, and support in entering the labour market;
- financial support for both families in work and families who are unable to work;
- services to tackle disadvantage and risk; and
- support for parents in their parenting (adapted from DWP, 2006).

Analysis by Hirsch (2006) for JRF and Harker (2006) for the Department for Work and Pensions (DWP) highlights successes in reducing workless households, in the tax credit system and in the introduction of the National Minimum Wage in reducing the numbers of children in poverty. Hirsch (2006, p 39) describes the reduction achieved as a 'historic reversal', but also discusses how those who remain out of work and on the margins of the labour market will require much more support than those who have already been helped. He also reveals how the tax credit system is more likely to take a lone parent out of poverty than a couple where only one person works. He argues that while work is the best route out of poverty, this does not mean that the solution to child poverty is for every parent to work. One reason for this is the impact of low pay and low-skilled work, with the labour market offering only limited opportunities to some; and the tax credits for those in work are insufficient to lift these families out of poverty. This 'underlying problem of in-work poverty' was also identified by Palmer et al (2006) in their analysis of progress in reducing poverty and social exclusion. In fact, their analysis identified a *rise* in the number of children in working families who are in poverty or who would be without tax credits. The government pledged to raise tax credits in line with earnings rather than prices, ensuring that relative poverty is addressed, but its own figures showed that in the first year (2003) Child Tax Credit was claimed by only 79% of those eligible (DWP, 2006). Its analysis did not reveal the characteristics of those who do not claim, but we know from other analyses of exclusion that they are likely to be among the most vulnerable and excluded families.

Harker (2006) also argues that policy around work and the labour market alone will fail to achieve the objective of reducing child poverty. Focusing on families for whom extra support in accessing work and in work-related benefits is required, she suggests that Jobcentre Plus (the DWP's local agencies responsible for supporting people in accessing the labour market) should take more of a 'family focus', supporting parents as parents so that they are able to work and fulfil the roles and responsibilities associated with their families. As Harker points out, half of all children living in poverty live in working households. The DWP has subsequently pledged to develop this family approach (DWP, 2007b).

Another perspective on this issue concerns the way in which policies may impact more broadly on family life. An overemphasis on work as a route to social inclusion can ignore the way in which parents, and in particular mothers, determine what is the right thing to do for their children and thus make different decisions about whether to take up full-time or part-time paid work, or to stay at home with their children. In her summary of the Care Values and Future of Welfare research programme, Williams (2004) identifies the way in which the values within different social networks can influence decisions about what is the right thing to do for children. A key conclusion arising from this research is that policies should be designed to support the different ways in which people seek to care for their children and that there is a need to balance an ethic of work with an ethic of care. This reflects the identification within the UNICEF (2007) study of children's experiences within their families as a necessary aspect of their well-being. Making time for parents to care for their children is as necessary as ensuring sufficient income and avoiding poverty.

The reductions in child poverty that the UK has seen since 1997 have not been equally distributed. Indeed, there were different starting points for different groups and policy has targeted different groups in different ways. One aspect of this concerns the geographical dimension of poverty. Recent analysis has demonstrated that, while overall poverty rates are falling, inequalities between geographical areas have increased since 1970 (although changes since 2000 are less clear) (Dorling et al, 2007). Both poor and wealthy households have become increasingly geographically segregated, with poverty clustering in urban areas. Thus, in light of the overall reductions in poverty outlined above, disadvantaged communities remain and it is less clear how work–related policy can impact on persistently poor groups. In London, poverty rose between 1999 and 2005, but the quarter reduction target was met in the regions of the North East, North West and South West. Poverty reduced at a greater rate in Wales and Scotland than in England, where there were much higher rates. The geographical concentration of disadvantage has led to a number of area-based initiatives by the New Labour government, such as Health Action Zones, Education Action Zones and the New Deal for Communities.

Hirsch's (2006) analysis reveals how the high incidence of lone parenthood and its close relationship to poverty in the UK resulted in the targeting of tax credits and increased state benefits at this group; as a result, the risk of a child in a lone-parent household being in poverty reduced from 61% to 48% from 1999 to 2005. Hirsch also identifies how children in families with under-fives have benefited as a result of the policy focus on them. However, large families (four or more children) have been identified as being particularly vulnerable to poverty, something explored in more length by Bradshaw et al (2006).

They point out that UK policy is not particularly sensitive to large families' needs. Although poverty in large families is falling as a result, Bradshaw et al conclude, of tax credits, 50% of children in these families are poor compared to 23% of single-child families.

In late 2007, a new 'Child Poverty Unit' was established by the DWP and the Department for Children, Schools and Families (DCSF) to explore how the child poverty target could be reached in light of Harker's (2006) review in particular. The 2008 Budget (the most recent at the time of writing) included an additional £1 billion for measures to reduce child poverty, although JRF estimates that £4 billion is required (JRF, 2008) with little information available about how measures beyond moving people into work might be identified and implemented.

Social exclusion in context

One implication of the analysis of social exclusion discussed in the first part of this chapter is that we need to understand the experiences of social exclusion in context and that such experiences will be different for different groups of children. In this section we apply this analysis of the different material, cultural and political dimensions of social exclusion to the circumstances and experiences of four groups of children who were among those targeted for action by the Children's Fund because of concern that they are at particular risk of poor outcomes in those areas that provided the focus for Children's Fund activity: educational performance and attendance, antisocial behaviour, health and access to services. In a survey carried out by the National Evaluation of the Children's Fund (Edwards et al, 2006), 88.3% of partnerships said that they targeted disabled children, 70.8% targeted black and minority ethnic children, 47.5% targeted Gypsy/Traveller children and 43.3% targeted refugee and asylum-seeking children, and these four groups are the focus of our analysis.

Material

The material dimensions of social exclusion relate both to income poverty and the impact this has on families' capacities to enable their children to take part in activities and have access to material goods that other children take for granted, and to the physical environments in which they live. There is little firm evidence about the extent of poverty among Gypsy/Traveller families, but Niner's (2005) study in one English region suggests that almost all residents on local authority sites are in receipt of Housing Benefit. Hirsh (2006) identifies Gypsies/ Travellers as one group consistently at risk of poverty. Niner's report suggests that some families live in significant poverty and parents interviewed for NECF, particularly those with large families, cited low income as key to their non-use of local leisure and recreational facilities. This is particularly significant in view of the poor quality of the physical environment in which many of them live, and the absence of safe space for play within caravans or on and around sites.

The material circumstances of families from black and minority ethnic groups vary widely, but those from black and minority ethnic backgrounds are more likely than the white population to be both poor and living in deprived areas. More than 50% of African Caribbeans and Africans and over 33% of South Asians (the groups most likely to be targeted by Children's Fund services) live in districts with the highest rates of unemployment (SEU, 2000). Children from black and minority ethnic groups are more likely to live in large families and thus are overrepresented among those missing out because policy does not adequately recognise the needs of large families. Indeed, one in five children in poverty is from a black and minority ethnic group, with rates for Black African, Pakistani and Bangladeshi children more than double the rate for white children. Measures targeting lone parents are less relevant to these groups, and those addressing in-work poverty are more relevant as nearly half of Pakistani and Bangladeshi children live in households with a single earner; current work-based policy is less sensitive to the needs of these families than others (Harker, 2006).

Most refugees come from the poorest countries of the world (UNHCR, 2002) and within the UK the new areas to which refugees and asylum seekers have been dispersed as a result of the 1999 Immigration and Asylum Act also tend to be characterised by poverty and relatively high levels of crime and antisocial behaviour. They are another group that Hirsh (2006) identifies as experiencing ongoing and persistent risks of poverty.

Material deprivation has a particular significance for families with disabled children. A majority of such families live in poverty or on the margins of poverty (Gordon et al, 2000) and the costs of raising a disabled child have been estimated at three times that associated with raising a non-disabled child (Dobson and Middelton, 1998). While families with disabled children are among those who have benefited from recent increases in financial support, they remain vulnerable to persistent poverty. Negotiating the benefits system can be time consuming and emotionally draining and this, combined with insufficient understanding of the benefits system on the part of service providers, can mean that families do not receive the support to which they are entitled. Disabled children often live in houses that are not adapted to their needs and this can have deleterious effects on their health, and on both the mental and physical health of their parents (Clarke, 2006).

Spatial

Spatial exclusions affect the four groups differently. Gypsies/Travellers live on the margins, out of sight of most of the settled population in places that have insufficient value to be required for other purposes. It can be argued that in this way the 'deviance' of the Gypsy/Traveller culture is less conspicuous (Sibley, 1995). While mobility between areas may be high, it is usually mobility between marginalised spaces. Mobility within the areas in which Gypsy/Traveller families settle temporarily is mediated by gender and age – while the men of the family may be out and about working, the women and children are often restricted to the site. Public transport facilities close to sites are poor or non-existent and taxi drivers hired to take children to sports and leisure centres by Children's Fund project workers are sometimes reluctant to do so (Mason et al, 2006).

With regard to refugees and asylum seekers, compulsory dispersal policies have resulted in asylum seekers being moved to areas of the country with limited experiences of receiving immigrant groups and this has limited asylum seekers' abilities to draw on supportive social networks (Woodhead, 2000; Sales, 2002). The 'bonding' social capital that is so important for marginalised groups is not available to them (Beirens et al, 2007) and an enforced mobility results in spatial exclusions in terms of both areas of residence and movement within areas.

In contrast, many more established families from black and minority ethnic communities live in areas with a high density of people from the same or similar communities, in some places, for example within areas in the West Midlands, constituting the majority population. This can lead to a strong sense of inclusion within the ethnic community, but a separation or segregation from the white population.

Physical barriers constitute a major factor restricting disabled children's access and mobility between spaces. It was evident from some of the data collected by NECF (Barnes et al, 2006a) that this could impact on expectations about what was possible – for example, a decision not to pursue a project based around swimming because the local pool did not have facilities to make this accessible to disabled people. Although some parents expressed preferences for their children to attend a special school, one consequence of this was that it was harder for children to take part in inclusive leisure activities because of the travel time to school, friendship networks linked to school and lack of knowledge about community-based opportunities. Thus, not only was there spatial segregation in education but this also impacted on children's relationships with their local neighbourhoods.

Access to goods and services

The Children's Fund sub-objective of improving access to services indicated that exclusion from services was recognised as a significant element of the social exclusion experienced by children and their families. But it is not only the specific design of individual services that can result in exclusion, some public policies have such negative impacts. For example, the 1994 Criminal Justice and Public Order Act, which repealed much of the duty of local authorities to provide and maintain sites for Gypsies and Travellers, has had a significant impact on relationships with the settled community. It has led to some Gypsies/Travellers building on sites without planning permission with a consequent increase in tensions in local relationships. Continual pressure on them to 'move on' has disrupted contacts with schools and other educational services and has affected both their physical and mental health. Hester (2004) shows how mainstream services are designed on the assumption of sedentary lifestyles and that there has been an historic reluctance on the part of public agencies to accept responsibility for ensuring the basic necessities of a safe place to live, appropriate education and health services for those who do not conform to this way of life. In addition, some schools are reluctant to accept Gypsy/Traveller children because of the anticipated impact on league table positioning, some Gypsy/Traveller parents who were themselves bullied at school are reluctant to expose their children to similar experiences, and a lack of trusting relationships between Gypsy/Traveller parents and teachers means that fears are hard to overcome (Kiddle, 1999).

Refugees and asylum seekers face particular difficulties in gaining access to services that most people take for granted. Limited interpretation services and information about eligibility mean that they often do not know about essential services and their rights to access them (Woodhead, 2000). Many mainstream services have poor levels of awareness of young refugees' and asylum seekers' and their families' needs, priorities and concerns (Beirens et al, 2006). Mobility resulting from dispersal and lack of knowledge of how things work can also affect access to the education system. The following have also been identified: delays in accessing schools as a result of oversubscription; schools' reluctance to accept young refugees or asylum seekers; their inability to offer appropriate support; and a belief that test performance would be adversely affected if they accept young refugees or asylum seekers (Audit Commission, 2000; Hek, 2005). The experience of some children in school is of limited understanding or capacity to respond to the impact of the traumatic events, loss and bereavement that some of them have faced (Beirens et al, 2006). Some children find it difficult to settle and their parents find it hard to support them because of their lack of understanding of the system and because of the challenges they are facing in meeting their own needs.

Racism is implicated in the way in which social exclusion is experienced by black and minority ethnic children and this is evidenced in particular in their experience of schools and of education. The rationale for many Children's Fund projects supporting black and minority ethnic children arose from concerns that black and minority ethnic pupils gain less benefit than their white peers from improvements in educational attainment (OfSTED, 1996; Warren and Gillborn, 2003). There is growing evidence that school-based processes are an important contributory factor in the production of poor outcomes for certain black and minority ethnic pupils (DfES, 2003a) and that practices such as behaviour management can have discriminatory effects (Blair, 2001). Black and minority ethnic pupils – particularly African Caribbean pupils – are vastly overrepresented in school exclusion figures (SEU, 1998a) and the SEU (2000) acknowledges that racial discrimination has a part to play in this. Black and minority ethnic children are also overrepresented in interventionist social care provision (Thoburn et al, 2004).

There are a number of factors that affect disabled children's access to services. Inadequate housing makes access to play and leisure facilities particularly important for disabled children, but both physical and attitudinal barriers impede access. Parents may be concerned about injury, low income and the attitudes of non-disabled children and adults, and these can act as barriers. Also, the inappropriate design of play equipment and the physical environments in which it is based act as a further barrier. Youth and play workers are rarely trained to support disabled children to make use of facilities that do exist. In spite of an increasing emphasis on effective coordination between service providers, families with disabled children often find themselves having to coordinate the services they receive from different providers.

Experiences of insufficiently integrated services relate to everyday frustrations such as coordinating hospital appointments with school timetables, and to more fundamental differences between agencies over agreed definitions, which can lead to resistance to joint working. These difficulties are particularly significant for families and children with complex needs (Watson et al, 2002). Although there has been a shift towards integrated schooling, education remains a site of dispute and the experience of poor performance in 'inclusive' education has prompted arguments to retain and halt the reduction of special schools. Davis and Watson (2001) have identified the way in which discourses around 'special educational needs' and a reiteration of 'difference' within school settings interact with structural and resource barriers to continue to generate disabling practices.

Health and well-being

The consequences of many of these experiences of exclusion affect the health and well-being of the four groups under analysis. For example, Van Cleemput (2000) highlights the links between deprivation, poor environments, lack of play facilities and poor health for Gypsy/Traveller children. Overcrowding, poor-quality housing, material poverty, poor diet and problematic access to health and social care services affect the physical and mental health of refugees and asylum seekers.

Cultural

For groups whose ethnicity, race or lifestyle places them outside the majority culture, an important dimension of the exclusion they experience relates to marginalisation, discrimination and stigmatisation. Official recognition of the existence of 'institutional racism' (Macpherson 1999) problematises the notion that policy responses to the experiences of black and minority ethnic children should be based on assimilating black and minority ethnic communities into the white host community. A similar point is made by Hester (2004) in relation to Gypsies/Travellers. In both cases the concept of 'exclusion' needs to be understood with reference to relationships with the majority society and does not necessarily describe experiences of black and minority ethnic or Gypsy/Traveller children in relation to their own ethnic or cultural groups.

Refugee and asylum-seeking children face similar problems of discrimination to other black and minority ethnic groups living in the UK and some parents interviewed for NECF reported being unwilling to let their children play outside because of the danger of harassment.

Gypsies/Travellers have been subject to persecution on racial grounds and on the basis of their lifestyles. Many travelling families have a strong cultural identity, but this can also place children apart from their peers because of the expectations about, for example, the role of girl children within the family and the acceptability of friendships with non-travelling children. Parents sometimes try to protect their children from bullying by maintaining their separation from 'mainstream' society. Van Cleemput's (2000, cited in Hester, 2004) observation that the discrimination experienced by Gypsies/Travellers would not be tolerated if applied to black or other minority ethnic groups indicates the depth of the distaste within the settled community for the Gypsy/Traveller lifestyle. Many of the groups that constitute 'Gypsies/Travellers' are outside the putative protection of anti-discriminatory legislation because they are not considered to have a distinct ethnic identity. Research has shown how those who do come within the terms of this legislation – English Gypsies and Irish Travellers – continue to face open hostility and discrimination. Sibley (1995) identifies the way in which stereotypes contribute to the processes by which these groups are pushed to the margins of society.

Hester (2004) argues that the dominant objective of recent policy has been that of assimilation – persuading, encouraging or coercing Gypsies/Travellers to give up their 'deviant' culture and adopt a more acceptable, sedentary lifestyle. Gypsies/Travellers who make the decision to pursue their own way of life are exercising a self-determination that sustains a collective identity necessary to resist the impact of the many exclusionary processes we have identified. From the perspective of the settled community and many mainstream services, this resistance can also be seen to contribute to 'self-exclusion' and this affected the design of some Children's Fund services that were intended to encourage engagement with 'mainstream' activities.

Self-determination and decision making

All children are subject to others making decisions on their behalf in important areas of their lives, such as which school to attend and whether or not to receive medical treatment, and by virtue of their age are not allowed to take part in certain activities, such as sexual activity or drinking alcohol. Although the age of criminal responsibility is lower in England than in many other European countries (10 in comparison with, for example, 14 in Germany, 16 in Spain and 18 in Belgium), the majority of the children within the remit of the Children's Fund are considered not to be responsible for actions that would be regarded in adults as criminal behaviour.

Nevertheless, the emphasis on children's participation within the Children's Fund and other recent policy initiatives is evidence that enabling children to be more active participants in taking decisions about matters that affect their lives is seen as one way of reducing social exclusion (NECF, 2004). Thus, the Children and Young People's Unit identified children and young people's participation as part of its core strategy as a cross-departmental unit: 'The Government wants children and young people to have more opportunities to get involved in the design, provision and evaluation of policies and services that affect them or which they use' (CYPU, 2001a).

The United Nations Convention on the Rights of the Child recognises that children have a right to be included in decisions about matters that affect them although it also acknowledges that children may be vulnerable and therefore also have a right to be protected. This recognition of vulnerability applies particularly to children defined as having 'special needs', but also applies to, for example, refugee children (particularly those who are unaccompanied) who are both vulnerable and subject to other people's decisions about where they can live and indeed whether they can remain in the country.

Conclusion

This discussion reveals the complexity of the processes involved in social exclusion and the inadequacy of theories of social exclusion based in the identification of individual or group risk factors. It also alerts us to the way in which policies and services can contribute to processes of exclusion – not only in terms of service design, but also in the cultural assumptions they make and in the extent to which they enable users or potential users to influence the nature of the help they receive.

This is an important starting point for an analysis of policies intended to improve child welfare and well-being and, more specifically, policies that adopt 'social inclusion' as an objective. It demonstrates the nature and extent of the challenge to be faced to respond to the multifaceted processes of exclusion. But social exclusion is only one concept that is relevant to an understanding of such policies and the practices they generate. In Chapter Three we move on to consider notions of risk and protection, and the way in which the family in general and parenting in particular have been co-opted as means towards the delivery of policy objectives.

Contemporary issues for preventative child welfare

Introduction

Social exclusion is a comparatively recent way of understanding the needs and experiences of children who are in various ways disadvantaged and, as we have seen, it is a perspective that has generated considerable controversy. However, the history of child and family policies demonstrates that controversy about the basis on which interventions and support should be provided is not new and has accompanied most attempts to develop policy and practice concerned with children's welfare and well-being. Given the inherent tensions between public matters and private lives, policy and practice responses to the needs of children and families have inevitably drawn on contested understandings of what constitutes effective interventions and desired outcomes. Childrearing and family life provoke considerable political and practice debate and preventative approaches within this context reflect the broader social policy tensions and competing discourses about state intervention in child and family life.

Historically, child welfare provision has, according to Fox-Harding (1997), been set within an analysis of the functions of the state when intervening in 'private' family life. Fox-Harding's analysis was concerned with the values accorded by state policy to family life and to childrearing capacity and the possible benefits of a range of social policy interventions. She suggested that childcare policies could be located within four possible perspectives – each reflecting a different set of values about the benefits and rights to state intervention in family life to promote childrearing. More recent academic analysis addresses the changing policy landscape and the emerging emphasis on longer-term economic and social outcomes for children. Social policy analysts have argued that the location of child welfare policies within an analysis of social exclusion represents a shift towards the theoretical framework of the 'social investment state' (Fawcett et al, 2004). Featherstone (2006) argued that this theoretical framework brings together social and economic projects concerned with the aims of economic viability and productivity. Usefully, Fawcett et al (2004) took the analysis of the social investment state developed by authors such as Giddens (1998) and Lister (2003) and explored how this is applied to children and to childhood. They suggested that there a number of dimensions to this:

- the development of strategies that are holistic, but also targeted;
- understandings of children as investments for the future rather than simply a concentration on current-well being;
- the forming of an alliance with parents (through mechanisms of support and control) to take forward the investment strategies; and
- a limited recognition of children as subjects in their own right, resulting in the emergence of ad hoc approaches to children's rights (Fawcett et al, 2004, p 4).

This analysis is a useful backdrop for understanding policy developments, specifically the changes in the paradigms of risk and protection and the discourses surrounding parenting and policy approaches that have started to emerge post Children's Fund for families at severe risk of exclusionary processes and poor outcomes.

Risk and protection in children's lives

The location of child welfare policies in a context of social exclusion has brought with it a political process of analysis to identify those deemed to be at risk of poor outcomes and therefore in need of early intervention and support to promote protective factors. Prevention has increasingly become linked to macro and micro understandings of risk and protective factors in relation to social exclusion. The New Labour development of generic child welfare strategies and specific national programmes concerned with attainment and well-being for all children (such as the Every Child Matters agenda discussed in Chapter Four) has encompassed responses for children who are particularly at risk of exclusionary processes and poor outcomes – because of where they live, their family environment or their own capacities. These children are seen to present real challenges to the political aspirations for socially and economically viable citizens, and as such, additional interventions have been proposed as necessary to ensure that the investment in childhood does deliver later benefits. For New Labour, the response to these 'at risk' children has repeatedly emphasised early interventions in family life through enhanced education and health provision.

As Chapter Two has described, children's pathways in and out of social exclusion are multifarious. However, New Labour has sought to identify those seen to be at most risk of poor outcomes and to target early interventions accordingly. This process of targeting reflects a policy assumption that early intervention in the lives of those displaying or experiencing certain conditions reduces the possibility of later, poor outcomes. Data about the impact of such approaches suggest a complex picture of inputs and outcomes. As France and Utting (2005) suggest, evidence supporting the paradigm of 'risk-focused prevention' in child welfare remains underdeveloped: 'Proponents of the paradigm acknowledge that there is much still to be learned about the influence of individual risk factors, including their salience at different stages in children's lives, and the ways that they interact and contribute to poor outcomes' (France and Utting, 2005, p 79).

The growing body of research about the impact of a range of variables on children's current and later performance presents a complex picture. The raft of preventative programmes launched by New Labour used varying analyses of risk and protective factors and, while these may or may not have been complimentary, they were all set within the paradigm described by France and Utting. Alongside this development of policy and programmes was research that demonstrated an uneven impact on outcomes for children from early intervention initiatives. Research nationally in the UK (National Evaluation of Sure Start, Research Team, 2005; Edwards et al, 2006) and internationally (see, for example, reports from the Canadian programme Better Beginnings, Better Futures, http://bbbf.queensu.ca/pub.html) suggested that those children who face the most difficult and enduring difficulties were the least responsive to the preventative programmes being developed. Despite this complex and uneven picture, early intervention/prevention policy developments have continued to secure considerable political commitment and have led to a significant shift in the context within which activity to enhance child welfare is being pursued.

The emphasis by New Labour on risk in relation to social exclusion and poor later outcomes, rather than risk as the assessment of the likelihood of a child suffering significant harm, created the opportunity for a new set of policy discourses to emerge about children and their families. Prior to the changes in the policy context for prevention, much of the debate about risk focused on either a forensic discourse concerned with investigation, assessment and treatment, or debates about how to address child and family support needs while responding to the pressing service demands of child protection. As Little et al (2003, p 209) noted, 'It is common to talk about a child being "at risk"....

This generally refers to a child who has been or is more likely than others to be maltreated'.

Since 2003, the mainstream understandings of 'at risk' have started to change. The risks articulated in contemporary policy are those concerned with children experiencing poor educational attainment, reduced social contribution, poor health and antisocial behaviour. As we have seen, these risks are seen to be experienced not only by children themselves, but as negative consequences for society as a whole.

The groups of children that historically have been the primary focus of state policies and practices – such as children in the public care system – are now included within the wider assault on factors that undermine child well-being and impede positive outcomes. The *Every Child Matters: Change for Children* (DfES, 2004a) policies set out core outcomes for children irrespective of their individual histories and circumstances. The relevance and usefulness of these outcomes for all children have been questioned:

> Every Disabled Child Matters (EDCM) is the campaign to get rights and justice for every disabled child. Disabled children, young people and their families have been left out for too long. EDCM is the campaign to put this right. We want all disabled children and their families to have the right to the services and support they need to live ordinary lives. (EDCM website: www.edcm.org. uk/Page.asp?originx_157qn_74514704196194n42n_ 2006911575g)

The children who were the subject of state concern are overrepresented in the groups experiencing poor outcomes and so the generic policies can be seen to be increasingly honed down to address specific groups. The argument here was that the generic outcomes agenda may not adequately reflect the needs of disabled children, and evidence elsewhere suggests that other groups such as black and minority ethnic children may also find the Every Child Matters outcomes wanting (Morris et al, 2006). Likewise, the specific and additional needs of young people within the care system were seen to merit particular attention through developments such as the Care Matters proposals (DCSF, 2007). This reflects the analysis by Fawcett et al (2004) of a move towards policy concerned with the needs of all children and the whole child, but within this, some groups receive particular attention: 'this approach does render certain groups of children and young people more visible, as recipients of both support and control strategies' (Fawcett et al, 2004, p 5).

This attempt within policy to respond holistically to the experiences of children also enabled expectations (moral and political) to be placed on all children and their families. Such expectations were seen as key to the promotion of protective factors. As with concepts of risk, concepts of protection also changed. A similar political and policy process occurred: past protective frameworks focused on individual needs in relation to safety and harm reduction; in contrast, current policy discourses emphasised protection through universal experiences of educational attainment, positive experiences of citizenship and robust networks of support and control. The previous context for child welfare was argued to be risk focused, paying little attention to strength-based models of practice (Parton 1997). Similarly, the current context could also be seen to be preoccupied with a different kind of risk:

> 'Protection' in this context is defined as something other than the opposite of risk. It refers, specifically, to factors that have been consistently associated with good outcomes for children growing up in circumstances where they are, otherwise, heavily exposed to risk. Less evidence is available about protection and its workings than about risk. (France and Utting, 2005, p 78)

For child welfare practitioners this introduction of new conceptual frameworks for risk, and to a lesser extent protection, created a series of tensions between historical responsibilities for children who may suffer significant harm, and new expectations for holistic responses to children and their families. The discourses of risk and protection were changing, and with this came new expectations and demands for professionals. Central to this was the legal and policy framework of the 2004 Children Act, which made explicit the expectations for multi-agency working, with early intervention and prevention part of the core activity of the new integrated children's services. We explore this development in detail in Chapter Four.

Parenting

As part of New Labour's preoccupation with the consequences of social exclusion and the incorporation of a political analysis of risk and protective factors into determining policy and practice, parenting styles and methods started to receive unprecedented attention. Historically, parenting had been seen to be the focus of state interventions, ensuring the well-being of children (for example the 1989 Children Act sought wherever possible to promote the upbringing of children by their parents and sought to articulate parental responsibility in law) and the focus of state intervention when found to be inadequate. Within the context of the social investment state, the focus on parenting skills became the means by which poor outcomes could be addressed:

> Parents and parenting have a profound impact on children's outcomes. Children tend to do well when parents have good relationships with them, have expectations of their behaviour, set boundaries and help them develop their own capacity to regulate their behaviour, have aspirations for them, believe in their ability to succeed and show it. Conversely, children's development can be held back and inhibited when parents are unable to offer their children these strong foundations, leading to disrespectful, antisocial behaviour, poor educational attainment and social exclusion. (Home Office, Press Release, 25 April 2007)

New Labour introduced a range of initiatives designed to support, educate or police parents. Sure Start offers a useful example: the services provided by Sure Start were rooted in understandings about the impact of early intervention on parenting and consequently on children's trajectories. The programme in its original form was specifically – and at times rigidly – targeted at those areas identified through local mapping as displaying high levels of need. The programme sought to have early contact with parents (through the development of integrated under-fives services) and to deliver a programme of early interventions that promoted child health, play and education, nurturing and parenting skills.

Other initiatives, while still utilising conceptual frameworks of risk and protection, placed different emphases on aspects of parenting. Funding was provided for the development of information and resource agencies such as the Family and Parenting Institute   funding streams aimed at developing highly targeted parenting interventions. (The latter included schemes such as the Family–Nurse Partnership scheme designed to deliver intensive early support to particular groups of pregnant women.) The Family and Parenting Institute suggested that it offered the opportunity to connect with parents' realities and by doing so provide the knowledge that will effect change:

> The Family and Parenting Institute is the leading centre of expertise on families in the UK. We do research and policy for the real world, provide practical resources for people working with families and find out what matters most to families.

> Over time the aim is to ensure that problems can be identified and responded to sooner by an expanded, skilled 'parenting workforce' so that eventually fewer families will require the more highly specialised, intensive and costly forms of 'help'. (Family and Parenting Institute: www. familyandparenting.org/research)

Within the developments described are implicit, and at times explicit, sets of understandings and judgements about 'good enough' parenting. The policy statements and guidance suggest a collective consensus about parenting – resulting in an 'othering' of those who either fail as parents or reject the normative parenting approaches considered necessary to preparing successful future citizens. Gillies (2005, p 75) argues that the emergence of parenting support as part of the policy drive for addressing exclusionary processes reflects a moral agenda concerned with conformity 'discourses of support are derived from a notion of obligated freedom, with interventions aimed at enforcing parenting norms and values'. She suggests that pervading New Labour's approach to parenting is the notion that poor parenting can be addressed through enhanced access to information and resources about parenting, that the key to change lies in failing parents being enabled to engage with mainstream values and knowledge. The development of initiatives such as the National Academy for Parenting Practitioners (DCSF, 2007) reflects this preference for supporting and promoting the management of knowledge about parenting. Gillies suggests that such activity detaches debates about parenting from concepts of social justice and poverty and allows the focus to be individual engagement with the opportunities presented by preventative programmes. Such analysis has important implications for the development of preventative services, and the focus of these services.

The conceptual framework of good parenting according to uniform standards is argued to be experienced as exclusionary and devaluing for those families who are either judged to have failed or cannot see their realities reflected in these policy discourses (Olsen and Clarke, 2003). Moreover, the failure to 'deliver' as parents is increasingly responded to in a punitive manner, with the introduction of new legal and policy frameworks that seek to enforce predetermined approaches to parenting. The behaviour of the child, specifically any antisocial behaviour, has become a means by which the parent is defined or responded to. Walters (2007) argues that dislocated parents have become the target of the risk agenda and their needs have become secondary to their responsibilities. Within this process of redefining parents as failing parents, both Walters (2007) and Gillies (2005) identify the separation of discussions about poverty from the discourses about the outcomes and processes of social exclusion.

Tisdall (2006) suggest that the construction of 'good' and 'bad' parents has been refined and enhanced by the growing body of legislation focused on antisocial behaviour and troublesome children.

While popular and political discourses of young people in trouble have consistently identified parents as a source of their child's antisocial behaviour, the power to place sanctions on them in order to address youth crime and offending has a more recent history. The 1982 Criminal Justice Act introduced measures to reinforce parental responsibility, but in practice the powers were never used. The 1991 Act revisited these ideas with three sets of powers: requiring parents to attend court with their children; making parents responsible for the payment of fines; and a duty on magistrates to bind over parents of children under the age of 16 to 'take proper care and exercise proper control over the child' (Section 58(2)(b)) (cited in Haines and Drakeford, 1998, p 151). New Labour governments have developed a range of programmes aiming to work with parents, including the Parenting Order that was introduced through the 1998 Crime and Disorder Act and under which parents must participate in a parenting support and education service. More recently, policy has been announced that targets pregnant women whose babies are deemed 'at risk' of social exclusion, as a means of reducing antisocial behaviour and the number of problem families from developing (*The Guardian*, 16 May 2007, p 1).

Any discussion of the emergence of political attention to parenting must note the translation of policy into practice. In the move from political rhetoric to service provision the evidence shows that parenting provision has become services that are concerned with mothers and women (Featherstone, 2006). As the data from various evaluations of parenting programmes has shown, the primary user groups are women, and indeed service provision is often built on this assumption. Women face a series of contradictory and complex political messages.

As Lister (2006) suggests, women's own well-being takes low priority in the New Labour policy push to augment income through women engaging in the labour market, while they are simultaneously the focus of programmes concerned with better parenting. Featherstone et al (2007) suggest that new developments in respect of engaging men as parents are long overdue – but bring with them complex issues about roles, responsibilities and gendered politics.

Families and children

Evidence on the impact of these preventative programmes and the approaches to parenting reveals a small but significant pattern of non-take-up of services and opportunities by what has been argued to be a number of families with enduring problems. (It is suggested that these families form 2% of all families, or 140,000 in number; Social Exclusion Task Force, 2007.) This group of families has caused New Labour considerable political concern – in 2006, Prime Minster Tony Blair suggested that 'some aspects of social exclusion are deeply intractable. The most socially excluded are very hard to reach. Their problems are multiple, entrenched and often passed down through generations' (Blair, 2006). This concern became even more evident when the Social Exclusion Unit (SEU) evolved into the Social Exclusion Task Force within the Cabinet Office during 2006. Rather than continuing to exist as a separate unit, the new group was designed to more deeply embed approaches to social exclusion within the work of other departments. It was suggested both that the SEU had become ineffective in terms of levering change and that it had become too open to influence by pressure groups (Wintour, 2006). Claiming positive results from the social policies of New Labour's first nine years of government in terms of increases in life expectancy and income and reductions in crime and child poverty, the task of the new group was now seen to address the problems of 'the persistent and deep-seated exclusion of a small minority' (www.cabinetoffice.gov.uk/social_exclusion_task_force/current_challenges). Four groups were identified as having the most problems, which endured over lifetimes and between generations:

- looked-after children;
- pregnancy teenagers;
- people with chronic mental illness; and
- families with complex problems – also referred to as 'high-harm, high-risk and high-lifetime cost' families.

This identification of a 'core' of what were argued to be failing families also created a set of political debates about engaging with the most marginalised of families. Welshman (2008) suggests that it is possible to see the lineage of these policy discourses in the concepts of transmitted deprivation explored by Keith Joseph in the 1970s. New Labour has adopted an assertive stance in relation to these families – seeking to couple opportunities to engage with mainstream society with sanctions and control. The SEU (2006) has carried out an analysis of multigenerational exclusion for the families seen to be failing their children, with poor outcomes being described as those transferred from adults to children within a family network; the SEU concern is with the disruption of this inheritance and the promotion of better outcomes.

Yet, within this political sphere, and indeed practice sphere, 'family' is often readily translated into 'parents', with two terms being used interchangeably. As Morris et al (2007) identified in their literature review of whole-family approaches, the literature concerned with family-based approaches to social exclusion is actually primarily concerned with parental activities and responsibilities. Policy and practice discourses rarely embrace extended family – the focus remains on parents, often mothers, who are seen as the principal means for promoting the desired outcomes in children. Thus, the concept of transferable exclusion between generations is translated into policy initiatives aimed at correcting flawed parenting, chiefly of mothers, to prevent children growing into socially excluded adults and subsequently replicating this process when they become parents.

The political concerns with troublesome families are further reinforced by the data and literature from a series of large-scale evaluations (such as of Sure Start and the Children's Fund), which suggest that there is evidence of non-take-up of both targeted services and open access services by families experiencing particular hardship. The review of the literature suggests limited knowledge about these families who are reluctant to use preventative provision (Morris et al, 2007), but also that the outcomes for those experiencing hardship and difficulties who use services may not be significantly different in some circumstances from those not taking up services (Sheppard, 2009).

The policy discourses adopted by New Labour can be argued to maintain and reinforce marginalisation through the images of family life that are represented. The notion of 'normal families' that are hard working and socially and economically connected to the mainstream brings with it the process of 'othering' those who fail to conform. Current policy agendas are increasingly concerned with the role of families in implementing central policies for parenting and childcare. Recent Social Exclusion Task Force publications have started to explore the role that families may play in maintaining or promoting inclusion/exclusion (the 'Think Family' series of publications: Social Exclusion Task Force, 2007, 2008). The most marginalised of families are the focus of specific policy responses, in particular those families seen to consistently generate poor outcomes for their children. However, as Levitas et al (2007) note, little if any data are drawn directly from the families who are the subject of these policy concerns, leaving a knowledge gap about the experiences and lived realities of marginalised families.

Evidence from a range of research (Marsh and Crow, 1998; Morris and Burford, 2006) demonstrates the importance of extended families in children's well-being. Yet, in both policy and practice, individuals are dislocated from their networks, with the emerging exception of 'high-harm, high-risk' families. In responding to the political concerns about what are perceived to be a small percentage of highly disruptive and socially excluded families, the policy discourse shifts from offering all children support in the Every Child Matters framework towards a highly interventionist approach explicitly underpinned by a moral agenda where the 'family' is the perceived unit of problem requiring forceful sanctions to ensure reintegration and social acceptability. The 'Respect' initiative launched by New Labour in 2004 in response to troublesome children, adults and families set out the following agenda:

Key measures of the Respect drive include:

- A new approach to tackling problem families through intensive family intervention programmes.
- A wide-ranging programme to address poor parenting. Additional investment will be available to fund parenting programmes across the country.
- Strengthening communities through more responsive public services. Local services will be encouraged to hold regular 'face-the-people' sessions.
- Improving behaviour and attendance in schools. Targeted action on persistent truants and a range of new measures to tackle poor behaviour in schools.
- The funding of constructive activities for young people such as youth intervention projects and sports programmes. (Respect Task Force, 2007)

This identification of a small group that both occupies a highly marginalised position and reproduces problems from one generation to the next marks a shift away from a structural analysis of the reasons for social exclusion and instead focuses primarily on the problems experienced and created by families considered to evidence poor parenting skills and chaotic interpersonal relationships. From this perspective, the policy emphasis of the Social Exclusion Task Force on improving tools that enable prediction and follow-up of those most at risk of exclusion, together with the promotion of budget-holding practitioners tailoring personalised programmes around those so identified (Social Exclusion Task Force, 2008), may be considered to offer a very partial response. The 'Guiding principles' of the Social Exclusion Task Force also emphasise multi-agency working, identifying 'what works' and highlighting best practice, and punishing underperformance in this area. Together with predicting who is most at risk and producing personalised programmes for these individuals and families, this is intended to support a continuing shift from 'treatment' to 'prevention'. The emerging responses to these families seek to cut across existing service divides, with the Family Pathfinder pilots launched in 2008 exploring integrated responses to families facing multiple difficulties (Social Exclusion Task Force, 2008).

The structural, material and attitudinal barriers faced by children, parents and families at risk of social exclusion are an important context for examining policy and practice responses to those considered to be 'difficult to reach', whether through mainstream or targeted services. Krumer-Nevo (2003) suggests that the term 'defeated families' is useful in understanding the lives of those families that are defeated both by their experiences and by the services that should be assisting them. The New Labour preventative initiatives have drawn on conceptual frameworks of risk, protection and early intervention, but the evidence reveals that the impact of such initiatives has been only partial, leaving some communities, groups and families marginalised and disengaged – and therefore defeated. The lens of family experiences is also adopted by Power (2007), who considers the lived experiences of families (in particular mothers and children) within cities, specifically within disadvantaged neighbourhoods. She, like Krumer-Nevo, argues that families are struggling against enormous difficulties to raise children and to survive the conditions that economic and social deprivations create. The central government analysis of 'hard-to-reach families' who fail to engage may not therefore reflect the reality of life as experienced by marginalised and social excluded communities and families, reinforcing their disconnection from mainstream policy discourses and representations.

Conclusion

This chapter has set out some of the key themes for children and their families that have emerged from New Labour's concern with the social and economic outcomes of social exclusion. Chapter Four considers specifically the development of preventative policy and practice in the fast-changing context generated by New Labour's drive to address social exclusion, and consequently to change the lenses through which family life is viewed. The advance of a political discourse that suggests, implicitly and explicitly, that there are right and wrong ways to approach parenting and family life brings with it important consequences for preventative policy and practice. Chapter Four explores these changes and sets the backdrop for the analysis of the learning coming from the Children's Fund that is presented in subsequent chapters.

FOUR

The development of preventative policy and practice: an overview

Introduction

A focus on social exclusion as a consequence to be avoided has led to a rethinking of the ways in which policies should be focused. The emphasis has shifted towards *preventing* harms arising, rather than adopting a primary focus of intervening once harms have become evident. This chapter describes this changing theoretical and policy approach to prevention in child welfare over the past four decades and sets these changes within the broader context of policy developments concerned with social exclusion and poor outcomes for children. Historically, policy understandings of prevention have drawn on service-led and needs-led models of prevention. These tiered frameworks for understanding prevention have categorised services according to the intensity of the need being met, or the focus of the services being delivered. Such frameworks have been widely adopted in England and Wales and have been used by service providers to identify the severity of the need or problem they are targeting and to justify the provision of various levels of intervention (DH, 2000). This chapter describes these tiered models of prevention and suggests that they are limited in their capacity to capture the contemporary context for prevention, one which is argued to locate prevention in the context of the risks posed by social exclusion (Morris and Barnes, 2008).

The evolution of child welfare policy: the refocusing debate and New Labour's response

The 1969 Children and Young Persons Act was a landmark in welfare policy for children and families. It provided local authority social workers and other nominated professionals with a wide range of powers to intervene in family life – with some opportunity for this intervention to be experienced as supportive rather than imposed. Evidence indicated that there was a growing level of formal intervention in family life, with the state intervening either to monitor inadequate parenting or to remove children from what were seen as dangerous or failing families (Parton, 1991). However, research exploring the experiences of children in the care system described a series of poor outcomes for children (DH, 1991). This research identified children who came from poor, fragmented families to be at far greater risk of state intervention – suggesting that social and economic characteristics of a child were as much an issue as any inherent risk within the family (Bebbington and Miles, 1989). This research exploring outcomes for children away from home encouraged a political and policy debate about achieving better outcomes for children – and particular emphasis was placed on supporting families and kinship care.

The scope for preventative provision within the 1969 Act was limited and the introduction of the 1989 Children Act alongside the commissioning and publication of a body of research during the early 1990s fuelled a debate about the focus of child welfare provision (DH, 1995). The research raised concerns about the overemphasis on child protection services at the expense of broader services to children in need of help and support. This research evidence revealed the extent to which children and their families accessed services through a series of assessments concerned with risk. Those demonstrating insufficient risk were often left to one side without alternative or helpful services (Gibbons et al, 1995), the risk being that families then re-entered the child welfare systems at a later stage with increasingly acute needs. Families also reported the absence of helpful early services, and described a requirement for a crisis to develop before local authority services could be accessed (Lindley, 1994). The economic and human consequences of this emphasis on high-risk situations led to what is often referred to as the 'refocusing debate': the challenges of supporting a shift towards prevention while simultaneously delivering services that met existing child protection responsibilities. This refocusing debate was widespread during the early 1990s, provoking extensive discussion within policy and practice communities (Rose, 1994).

The development of the 1989 Children Act was, in part, informed by these concerns about early intervention and support. The 1989 Act placed a set of expectations on child welfare providers to provide supportive services to children who were assessed as being 'in need'. The emphasis of the child welfare policies at this time was on recognising and assessing the needs of individual children and their families (Part III of the 1989 Act) and responding accordingly to the identified level of need or risk. The Act's guidance made considerable use of the concept of 'partnership', suggesting that social work should seek to negotiate and include families wherever possible in the service their children

received. However, the concept of a 'child in need' was open to debate
– the Act suggests that:

> For the purposes of this Part a child shall be taken to be
> in need if—
>
> (a) he [sic] is unlikely to achieve or maintain, or to have the
>   opportunity of achieving or maintaining, a reasonable
>   standard of health or development without the provision
>   for him of services by a local authority under this
>   Part;
> (b) his health or development is likely to be significantly
>   impaired, or further impaired, without the provision for
>   him of such services; or
> (c) he is disabled. (1989 Children Act, Section 17[10])

The Act therefore suggested that a child in need was identified by
setting their progress against the progress of children not seen as 'in
need'. The intention underpinning the legislation was that 'children
in need' would be able to access helpful negotiated services (Tunstill,
1997), with an expectation that families be supported and children
remain within their families wherever possible (Section 17[1]). In
reality, the implementation of the Act largely failed to address the needs
of children unless they were assessed as at risk of significant harm.
The evidence showed that local authorities had developed eligibility
criteria for accessing services for children in need in such a way as
to focus services on children at risk of harm, with children who had
low level or chronic needs receiving few if any services (Aldgate and
Tunstill, 1995).

New Labour therefore inherited a legal framework that was
permissive in terms of the provision of early support services before
significant harm occurred. But the implementation of the legislation
and its accompanying guidance had placed the emphasis of activity
on children at risk of harm and needing child protection services.
Not long after entering office, New Labour instigated a series of
cross-cutting reviews, in part as a result of the Social Exclusion Unit's
(SEU's) 1998 report on Neighbourhood Renewal (SEU, 1998b). There
were 18 reports by Policy Action Teams (PATs), and these became
known as the PAT reports. The focus of the majority of these reports
was matters directly linked to communities – employment, housing
and skills. However, within this series of reports, attention was also
given to children and young people and the PAT 12 report reviewed

services for young people described as 'at risk'. This report made the conceptual shift away from children at risk simply being children in need of protection. Instead, the report was concerned with broader issues of poor outcomes in relation to homelessness, drug use, crime, literacy, pregnancy and worklessness. The PAT 12 report argued that both the construction of the 1989 Act and its implementation had significant shortcomings:

> PAT believes the philosophy which lay behind the Children Act 1989 has never been put into practice for a combination of reasons:
>
> - the fact that the costs of crisis intervention fall on different budgets from those that might fund earlier preventative activity – and services that might fund earlier preventative activity would not receive any payback from it
> - the way the priorities for services for young people are set out in legislation and policy guidance, and the consequences this has for their deployment of resources and
> - professional cultures. (SEU, 2000, p 76)

This PAT report and the policy developments that emerged in response across the range of child welfare provision stimulated a shift of focus from 'children in need' towards an extended concern with 'children at risk of social exclusion' as a result of factors believed to be connected with social exclusion such as neighbourhoods, education and employment (Morris, 2004). Furthermore, the work of the SEU had drawn attention to the relatively poor outcomes for young people in the UK when set against other European Union (EU) countries (see also the United Nations Children's Fund's report discussed in Chapter Two; UNICEF, 2007).

As a result of this policy shift, the emphasis of the refocusing debate on redirecting individualised services can be argued to have become redundant. Instead, political attention was being given to the development of large-scale preventative programmes, primarily Sure Start, the Children's Fund and Connexions. The PAT 12 report identified the outcomes and challenges for young people at risk of social exclusion and built on the thinking and commentary in the consultation document *Supporting Families* produced by the Home Office (1998). The PAT 12 report identified gaps in preventative services for children and young people and argued for a greater emphasis on early intervention, more flexibility on the part of service providers and increased coordination of local provision in order to address the complex needs of vulnerable children and young people who were seen to be at risk of the consequences of social exclusion.

In 2000, the death of Victoria Climbié (a child cared for by relatives who died as a consequence of severe cruelty and neglect) resulted in a wide-ranging review of children's services led by Lord Laming. The inquiry was considered to be a primary driver for 2004 legislation concerned with children's services – the 2004 Children Act. However, Parton (2006) argued that the introduction of the Act was only in part a response to the death of Victoria Climbié. He suggested that there was evidence of important policy moves that, aside of Lord Laming's recommendations following Victoria Climbié's tragic death, gave the impetus for change in the emphasis and remit of children's services. The recommendations of the PAT 12 report heralded these later developments in approaches to prevention and early intervention. The PAT 12 themes of early intervention and multi-agency responses to the consequences of social exclusion became established in the policies that emerged in the following years. Consultation documents such as *Every Child Matters* (DfES, 2003b), the introduction of the 2004 Children Act and accompanying guidance facilitated this shift towards addressing more broadly the needs and experiences of children: 'The vision we have is a shared one. Every child having an opportunity to fulfil their potential. And no child slipping through the net' (DfES, 2004b, p 5).

The key characteristics of policy relating to child welfare at this point are thus, first, the integration of those who are marginalised, and second, the disruption of negative trajectories among those identified as at risk of becoming socially excluded in order to promote outcomes that ensure longer-term productivity, cohesion and social inclusion (NECF, 2004).

The delivery of preventative services

Before exploring how prevention has been conceptualised within these changes in child welfare policy, we consider how preventative services have been delivered, and the effect that changes in political emphasis and structures have had on the nature and organisation of services. Traditionally, preventative services sat within a range of providers – health, social care, education and the voluntary sector. The services that did exist to prevent harms arising (and these were argued to be limited) sat within agencies and organisations that delivered their services independently of each other with little if any joint working. Prior to New Labour's first term of office, local arrangements for children's services did experience some change within each 'silo' with the intention of trying to ensure better coordination across services, but the real change across the system as a whole came with New Labour's drive for wholesale transformation. The introduction of the 1989 Children Act brought with it expectations of inter-agency cooperation, but in reality limited cross-agency activity was developed. Expectations of degrees of inter-agency working had long been established in the context of child protection, although the evidence from child death reviews and serious case reviews continued to indicate that the levels of cooperation and joint working were insubstantial and ineffective (DH, 2002).

New Labour therefore inherited a relatively fragmented set of arrangements for preventative children's services both locally and nationally. Within this picture, the role of the voluntary sector was uneven, and at times unknown. The social exclusion analysis emphasised the multidimensional nature of problems experienced by disadvantaged children and families and responses required similarly multi-agency solutions. Thus, the emergence of social exclusion in New Labour's approach to child welfare was accompanied by changes to central and local frameworks for delivering preventative and targeted services.

> Central to these changes has been the requirement on statutory agencies to work with each other, and with voluntary and community and sometimes private sector agencies, in order to develop and implement strategies capable of addressing such problems holistically. The government has required the creation of local level partnerships to address issues such as crime and community safety, neighbourhood renewal and health inequalities, as well as children and young people. (Edwards et al, 2006, p 11)

The government's multifaceted attack on social exclusion was characterised by swiftly changing policy requiring changes in practice as a series of large-scale and small-scale preventative initiatives were announced. This was a turbulent period. Developments within the statutory sector sat alongside a growing emphasis on the role of the voluntary sector in the local delivery of preventative provision.

In 2001, joint guidance was issued by the Department of Health, the Department for Education and Employment, the Department for the Environment, Transport and the Regions, the Home Office, the Department of Culture, Media and Sport, HM Treasury and the Cabinet Office. It stipulated new advice on the joint planning of services for children and young people. As a result, Children's and Young People's Strategic Partnerships (CYPSPs) were formed in each local authority area to develop Children and Young People's Strategic Plans. These strategic partnerships involved the statutory, voluntary and community sectors, and were also charged with considering the views of children and young people.

The announcement of CYPSPs was preceded by the announcement in the same year of Local Strategic Partnerships (LSPs). Local Strategic Partnerships were expected to include representatives of statutory, voluntary, community and independent sectors as well as community representatives, and were tasked with producing a strategic plan for the whole of the local authority area. This overarching community plan was to sit above all strategic working, and would inform and be informed by the planning undertaken in locally based and thematic initiatives. The position of LSPs was clarified by guidance issued in late 2002 requiring all upper-tier and unitary authorities to bring together all those responsible for planning, commissioning and delivering all services for children from birth to young people aged 19. The remit was to develop a Local Preventative Strategy.

As described in detail later in this chapter, the *Every Child Matters* Green Paper (DfES, 2003a) and the subsequent 2004 Children Act contained a series of themes that had a direct bearing on the delivery of preventative services. The Act sought to enhance the integration of services and to enable intervention in children's lives before crisis points were reached. The Green Paper included the announcement of the creation of Children's Trusts. These were locally integrated arrangements for the joint delivery of services to children and families – and included Education, Social Services, Leisure and – in some areas – Health. However, initial resistance from some local authorities to a specified local management and service structure led to the development being scaled down to 'Children's Trusts or other integrated arrangements'. Some 35 pilot trusts were set up to run for three years. Following the introduction of the 2004 Act, these pilots became part of a wider picture of integrated children's services – with the merger of social services and education departments and the forging of partnerships with health agencies. Local authorities were expected to deliver children's services through integrated structures and this was mirrored at a national level by the creation in 2007 of the Department for Children, Schools and Families (DCSF). The 2004 Act also introduced the Children and

Young People's Plan, which laid out the guidance for the development of integrated planning and delivery.

Financial arrangements also became increasingly integrated. In 2005 Local Area Agreements (LAAs) were introduced as a means of local authorities being able to pool streamed budgets and to arrive at joint working arrangements for the delivery of services attached to these budgets. For some voluntary and community sector organisations, this caused concern – the LAAs were led by the statutory sector and funding streams such as the Children's Fund that might previously have sat within the voluntary sector were now managed by the local authority. The concerns articulated by the third sector focused on the loss of local diversity in the desire for streamlined arrangements.

The introduction of Children's Centres in 2005 – aiming to provide an integrated service for children and families in disadvantaged areas, targeting the needs of children under five years of age and seeking to work in partnership with local voluntary agencies – was a further integrated initiative. The Extended Schools programme was another new development prompted by New Labour's interest in joined-up responses and 25 'Pathfinders' were announced in autumn 2003. This initiative sought to allow schools to develop into community resources so that they could become a base for a range of activities and services to meet the needs of its pupils, their families and the wider community. All local authorities received funding by 2006 for such developments and schools faced a series of policy expectations to offer extended services based on inter-agency collaboration.

The 2004 Act thus stimulated widespread change in local arrangements. More recently, in 2007 the DCSF issued the 'Third Sector Strategy and Action Plan' (DCSF, 2007), which sought to identify the role and value of the third sector, and to promote the involvement of the third sector in local preventative services.

Despite this picture of fast-changing policy with multiple new developments, the evidence from within the UK and elsewhere continued to suggest that children in the UK faced a series of challenges and barriers – and were failing to reach the levels of achievement or happiness experienced by their peers in other countries (UNICEF, 2007). This in part provoked a further central government initiative in 2007 – the Children's Plan, which rearticulated the core New Labour themes: responsive services that crossed boundaries and promoted early intervention and prevention.

A focus on prevention and how services should be planned, designed, governed and delivered to achieve this has thus been at the heart of rapidly changing central prescriptions for child and family policy, and government has issued substantial guidance to local agencies on this topic. Amid all this change, three general themes emerged:

- first, *the desire to drive forward integrated services* – through planning service provision and social care education (the piloting of new integrated qualifications in social care began in 2006). The extent to which these developments will impact on outcomes for children in the longer term is as yet unknown (Morris, 2008). Early evidence suggests that the focus for professionals is working relationships and, while families appreciate the reduced burden of multiple interventions, there is limited evidence of the need or reason for the service being changed (Sloper, 2004; Frost, 2005);
- second, *the vulnerable nature of the third sector involvement in preventative services*. Earlier initiatives such as the Children's Fund that sought to lock in voluntary agencies to the partnerships developed to deliver the work of the Fund were replaced by local authority-led arrangements such as LAAs. Concerns about how the third sector would play a role resulted in specific guidance being issued. However, tensions continue about the role of the voluntary sector, with the desire for common outcomes and approaches set against the unique contributions of small community-based groups that are able to be flexible and develop ways of working specific to particular needs and circumstances (Morris et al, 2006; NCVCCO, 2008);
- third, *the limited capacity for learning to flow across policy and practice developments*, a consequence of the speed of change and the layering of change onto change. As we have seen, New Labour commissioned a series of large-scale national evaluations, each attached to preventative initiatives: the New Deal for Communities (targeting communities in disadvantaged areas), Health Action Zones (focusing on enhancing health outcomes in high-need areas), Education Action Zones (seeking to promote better educational outcomes) and the Children's Fund and Sure Start (both aiming to address the impact of social exclusion on later outcomes for children). The evaluations attached to each initiative produced detailed reports, but the evidence indicates that attempts nationally and locally to 'join up' the emerging learning were limited, with some evaluations demonstrating an absence of any links with other national evaluations (Barnes et al, 2001; Edwards et al, 2006).

More locally, learning was inhibited by the perceived legitimacy and/or stability of an initiative. Edwards et al (2006) argued that the learning gained from the Children's Fund by other local policy makers and providers was limited by the positioning of the initiative. Those Children Fund partnerships that sat within established local structures and systems were able to influence local activity but also tended to be less innovative. The partnerships that were less well connected and somewhat marginalised were able to be more creative, but paid a price in terms of the exchange of knowledge and learning. There is little doubt that the evaluation findings and learning emerging from each of the large-scale evaluations resonated with previous learning from other evaluations, but New Labour in its haste to drive forward the change agenda failed to join up the learning, despite seeking to join up the services.

Every Child Matters: Change for Children

As part of its wide-reaching reform of children's services, in 2003 the government introduced the concept of universally shared outcomes regardless of individual needs and experiences. In the Green Paper *Every Child Matters* (DfES, 2003b), five outcomes were introduced and identified. These were commonly known as:

- being healthy;
- staying safe;
- enjoying and achieving;
- economic well-being; and
- making a positive contribution.

These outcomes and the accompanying Green Paper (DfES, 2003b) embodied a commitment to take forward the preventative agenda and the-then Minister for Children, Margaret Hodge, argued that the development of these shared outcomes reflected New Labour's commitment to arrive at better outcomes for *all* children – moving away from the previous policies of targeted outcomes for specific groups (such as children in the public care system or young offenders). The Every Child Matters consultation document (DfES, 2003b) was presented as an important opportunity for services to children to be joined up and for early intervention to be a central part of mainstream services.

The five outcomes were argued to have their origins in a process of consultation with children, young people and their families. *Every*

Child Matters: Change for Children (DfES, 2004a, p 8) suggested that: 'The five outcomes for children and young people are given legal force in the Children Act 2004, as the components of well being and the purpose of co-operation between agencies. They are central to the programme of change'.

The guidance from the Department for Education and Skills (DfES) supporting the Every Child Matters outcome implementation goes on to translate the broad outcomes into a detailed chart of indicators, performance targets and child-specific outcomes (DfES, 2005). These replaced the outcomes that initiatives which predated the Change for Children agenda had adopted. Part of the local task therefore became the mapping across from existing outcomes (such as those set for Sure Start and the Children's Fund) to the new outcomes. Williams (2004) suggested that the development and wholesale promotion of the Every Child Matters outcomes reflected a policy shift away from leaving children and childcare hidden within families – unless troubled or troublesome – towards having a central and highly visible role in policy. However, she also critiqued this development, arguing that some of the changes envisaged lacked the necessary robust vision and values framework. She cited a specific tension in the relationship between the child-level strategies and outcomes and the broader generic strategies to address risks and promote well-being. Williams suggested that what was absent in the Green Paper (DfES, 2003b) were the principles to underpin the changes, arguing that the failure to engage with a debate about the values that should guide and inform policy development – such as trust and respect – was a missed opportunity. But this difficulty in the translation of wide-ranging intentions into change for individual children was not new to the Green Paper. The Children's Fund (which predated the Green Paper) had also set out a wide-ranging overarching objective to promote pathways out of poverty through joined-up support and early intervention. The translation of this objective into child-level outcomes saw the emphasis shift from broad social and economic concerns to a focus on individual child-level attainments in education, health and behaviour. The fact that this apparent commitment to address the structural factors that contribute to the exclusion of children living in disadvantaged circumstances can be subverted into practices designed to enhance individual performance underpins many of the critiques of the social exclusion discourse discussed in Chapter Two.

Within the Every Child Matters framework for children's services there were new and enhanced roles for mainstream providers. In particular, through the Extended Schools initiative the education system was expected to play a core role in supporting children and their families at risk of social exclusion, offering extended care and services tailored to local needs. As discussed earlier in this chapter, this development sat within the framework of integrated children's services – initially piloted as Children's Trusts with expectations that local authority child-focused services (for example education, social services, some aspects of health provision) became part of a unified structure (DfES, 2004b).

The emphasis on prevention and early intervention has continued throughout New Labour terms of office. Within this has been a political desire to maintain a commitment to 'joined-up' provision that seeks to address from an early stage children's potential poor outcomes. However, as we discussed in Chapter Three, despite having established a range of national preventative programmes that were subsequently moulded into the Every Child Matters outcomes framework, the evidence continued to suggest that those who experienced enduring and chronic risks of social exclusion failed to respond to such initiatives. As a result of these concerns, increasingly targeted initiatives have been developed. In 2006, a series of small-scale highly focused preventative initiatives was piloted, including schemes targeting 'high-risk' first-time parents (usually mothers) and families with multiple problems (Social Exclusion Task Force, 2007). These projects sat alongside wide-ranging consultation documents such as *Youth Matters* (DfES, 2006), which sought to identify and target those young people facing particular difficulties or presenting specific needs within the generic outcomes framework.

The 2007 Children's Plan continued to place heavy emphasis on education and integrated services as vehicles for achieving change for children (DCSF, 2007). Announced as a major overhaul of approaches to children and children's services, the Plan actually built on and further extended existing policy streams. It also sought to articulate the role parents and families could and should play in promoting better outcomes for children. Some groups, such as disabled children, received specific attention and there was also an acknowledgement that the most marginalised of children and families had felt relatively limited effect from the preventative programmes previously developed. The proposed ways forward – further enforcement of joined-up working, the enhanced use of education as a vehicle for change and the double-edged message of support for parents who engage and conform – maintained the policy discourses that have run throughout New Labour's terms of office.

Understandings of prevention in child welfare

In spite of the continuing and evolving emphasis on prevention in policy and practice, there is limited evidence of the development of more sophisticated theoretical frameworks for interpreting and analysing preventative approaches. The frameworks for understanding preventative child welfare provision in the UK have for the past decade regularly utilised the conceptual framework developed by Hardiker et al (1989, 1991). In this framework Hardiker et al sought to consider the strategies for delivering preventative services in relation to theoretical understandings of the welfare state. This enabled an analysis of the choices that could be made about the aims and activity of preventative provision to be framed within a discussion of the extent to which the state accepted responsibility for ensuring the welfare of children.

Within Hardiker et al's analysis of the welfare policy contexts for preventative services, provision was categorised into four tiers: primary, secondary, tertiary and quaternary. Briefly, Hardiker et al argued that it was possible to see links between the different emphases of preventative provision and different theoretical understandings of the welfare state. They suggested that a welfare state that accepts society as essentially unequal and sees these inequalities as important drivers within a free market economy (*the residual model*) would support welfare provision only as the last resort for families with significant weaknesses. Consequently, the state would support preventative provision that was highly focused and operated with restrictive eligibility criteria. A welfare state that seeks to promote and maintain the status quo would see preventative services as necessary in supporting the integration of families and reducing the difficulties families may experience (*the institutional model*). In contrast, a welfare state that promotes state provision as an important tool in addressing inequalities would support extended preventative services that are fully accessible and designed for open access (the *developmental model* and the *radical/conflict model*). There are clear differences in Hardiker et al's analysis between the last two models – primarily in the extent to which provision is used to promote and support social change.

This analysis indicates that preventative social work and other welfare interventions can have many forms and purposes. Thus, the view that only activity that can be placed in the primary or secondary levels of prevention can be justified as truly preventative should be rejected. Crucially, Hardiker et al (1989, p 355) argued that: 'Our hypothesis is that it is consideration of the value base underlying the intervention which helps towards greater conceptual clarity about preventative work.

The adoption by policy makers in the late 1990s of Hardiker et al's work saw a dilution in the original linking of preventative activity with the theoretical analysis of the welfare state. Instead, a partial representation of this work was adopted, which focused simply on the tiered model of prevention. In the process of this dilution of the original analysis, important opportunities for understanding the context and overall intent of preventative activity were lost. As a result, the focus of policy and practice analysis became the type of service and intensity of the problem, rather than exploring assumptions about the rationale for provision and the intended outcomes. It was this tiered model of provision that became the framework that many mainstream service providers used to assess their activity (DH, 2001) during the early years of implementing the 1989 Children Act.

It was also evident in the thinking that influenced the design of the Children's Fund:

> Level One: Diversionary. Here the focus is before problems can be seen – thus prevention strategies are likely to focus on whole populations.
>
> Level Two: Early prevention implies that problems are already beginning to manifest themselves and action is needed to prevent them becoming serious or worse.
>
> Level Three: Heavy-end prevention would focus on where there are multiple, complex and long-standing difficulties that will require a customisation of services to meet the needs of the individual concerned.
>
> Level Four: Restorative prevention focuses on reducing the impact of an intrusive intervention. This is the level of prevention that would apply to, for example, children and young people in public care, those permanently excluded from school or in youth offender institutions or supervision and/or those receiving assistance within the child protection framework. (CYPU, 2001b, p 37)

An emerging approach to child welfare policy that apparently focused on the multidimensional experience of social exclusion and its consequences for children's lives, was therefore being implemented through the application of models of prevention that were concerned with the intensity of need and the type of the service to be provided in response to this (Morris and Spicer, 2003). Such models made little if any reference to the intended outcome in relation to inclusionary/ exclusionary processes, or the understandings being utilised about the relationships between the child, family, community and state. Hardiker et al's early work (1989), which analysed the way in which different conceptualisations of prevention reflected substantially different beliefs about the role of the state in delivering child welfare, was thus co-opted for a very different purpose. Analysis of prevention became service and process led, with little reference to the purpose and function of prevention within an analysis of state intervention in family life.

National preventative initiatives

As political attention concentrated on preventing the perceived consequences of social exclusion, New Labour rolled out a series of cross-cutting initiatives that sought to deliver early intervention aimed at disrupting the potential pathways of children into social exclusion. The first of these, and the largest, was Sure Start. In 1997 the government announced the development of the Sure Start programme as part of that year's Comprehensive Spending Review, and its arrival was discussed in the Supporting Families document (Home Office, 1998). The programme was heralded as a key political flagship for new ways forward, and it was argued that the early thinking underpinning Sure Start was radical in being both directed towards joined-up provision and evidence based (Glass, 1999).

The programme drew heavily on American early intervention programmes, such as Head Start, and targeted children aged four years and under who were living in areas where there were significant risks of poor outcomes associated with social exclusion. The size and scale of the programme reflected the nature of the political commitment to early intervention – the first tranche of funding was £540 million, with significant additional funding being made available as the programme was developed. The early plans located 200 Sure Start projects in areas of high need, with 'wrap-around' services that met young children's health, social and emotional needs, and the parenting development needs of their carers. Glass (1999) argued in these early stages that the programme was effectively linked with other cross-cutting developments (such as the New Deal for Communities) and this would therefore reinforce the preventative agenda by linking it with initiatives concerned with broader social and economic regeneration. However, despite only the partial completion of the associated National Evaluation (the National Evaluation of Sure Start known as NESS) and the local projects still being in early stages of development, by 2001 policy decisions were made to broaden and amend the focus of the programme. The consequences of these changes were also described by Glass – one of the original architects of the programme who went on to be a key critic of its changing focus of activity – as follows:

> My view – and I argued it at the time when I was in the Civil Service and I have argued it subsequently – was that we should have learned much more about the experience from those 200 before we rolled it out on any scale. I do feel that we have rolled it out on the basis of inadequate evidence about how best it should be done as much as whether it has an effect, and being clear about the kinds of impact we wanted this programme to have.... We rolled it out too much, too fast and too inadequately reviewed. (Glass, evidence to the Select Committee on Science and Technology (Minutes of Evidence), 24 May 2006)

Glass suggested that the rapid changes to the breadth and focus of the programme significantly diluted the capacity of Sure Start to achieve change for children at risk of social exclusion and for the impact of the programme to be adequately assessed. The remit of Sure Start since 2006 has been far wider than early plans envisaged and now seeks to support childcare provision, promote the return to work of parents, deliver through Children's Centres various preventive services and roll out the original principles of Sure Start across all local authorities. The age range for the programme has also been amended to meet the needs of a wider group of children. This has substantially changed the original brief and activity of Sure Start and embedded it tightly within New Labour's drive to connect economic projects with welfare projects (this analysis was explored in Chapter Three).

As we have already touched on in preceding discussions, a further major preventative initiative emerged as a result of the PAT 12 cross-cutting review of children at risk initiated by New Labour. The Children's Fund was developed to respond to a perceived shortfall in preventative provision for children aged five to 13 years. The Children's Fund was created following the 2000 Comprehensive Spending Review. It had a total budget of £960 million and ran from 2001 to 2008. Its creation was set within the New Labour commitment to address child poverty and social exclusion and its aim was described as follows: 'The Children's Fund is a central part of the Government's agenda for children and families and aims to make a real difference to the lives of children and young people at risk of social exclusion' (CYPU, 2001b, p 2).

As with Sure Start, emphasis was placed on responding to children who demonstrated particular risks of poor outcomes linked to social exclusion. However, whereas Sure Start interventions were argued to be evidence based, and were relatively structured in the project's design, the Children's Fund was a more open funding stream that allowed local area multi-agency partnerships to determine both the focus for activity in terms of groups targeted (see Chapter Five) and the ways in which they would respond to the needs and circumstances of these groups (Chapter Six). The expectation was that each local authority area would develop a Children's Fund partnership that would include local authority agencies, the voluntary and faith sectors, representatives of children and family organisations and other relevant local bodies. The Fund was expected to develop plans in consultation with children and young people and to work within the three conceptual pillars of partnership, participation and prevention (CYPU, 2001b). The initiative was firmly rooted in the discourse of risk and protective factors, which, as we have seen, was a key feature of New Labour's child welfare policies at this time.

The Children's Fund Guidance (CYPU, 2001b) for partnerships was premised on a broad and underdeveloped understanding of risk and protective factors. Reflecting perhaps France and Utting's (2005) analysis, which suggested that little is understood about the interplay between risk and protective factors (see Chapter Three), the Guidance did not specify protective factors at all, instead stating simply that they are factors that 'may ameliorate' the negative effects of risk factors (CYPU, 2001b, p 39). The outline of risk and protective factors and how these should be used to profile areas and highlight areas of need, and how assessment of young people should be based on this framework, took two and half pages and was placed within an Annex to the Guidance. The Guidance focused entirely on risk factors, and placed these within the three domains of community, family and children. The fourth sphere within which risk factors have been identified – school – was not referred to in the Guidance, in spite of the level of consensus about its significance among proponents of the risk and protection analysis (France and Utting, 2005; YJB, 2005).

A smaller programme than Sure Start, but still with a national remit, the Children's Fund encountered a particularly unstable and difficult political context. The programme was managed in its early years by the Children and Young People's Unit (CYPU), a cross-departmental unit aimed at raising the profile of children and young people across central government. Further turbulence was caused in 2004 when the CYPU was itself disbanded, resulting in the coordination of the Children's Fund being assumed by the Department for Education and Skills, which had itself newly absorbed a broad range of responsibilities for children's services.

The original Guidance provided an overarching objective for the Children's Fund:

> to provide additional resources over and above those provided through mainstream statutory funding, specific programmes and through specific earmarked funding streams. It should engage and support voluntary and community organisations in playing an active part and should enable the full range of services to work together to help children overcome poverty and disadvantage. (CYPU, 2001b, p 6)

This broad objective was translated into a series of seven sub-objectives that focused on individual child attainments in health, education and antisocial behaviour, alongside two sub-objectives concerned with child and family satisfaction and family and community involvement in the services.

However, within a relatively short period of time, the decision was made by the ministers linked to the CYPU that the initiative should devote 25% of its funding to addressing crime and antisocial behaviour. This change of emphasis caused considerable local disquiet within Children's Fund partnerships, and this unease was reinforced by a subsequent decision to reduce overall spending on the programme. Both decisions were later diluted as a response to the instability caused within local authorities and the voluntary sectors by these original changes in policy and funding. This fast-changing and unstable policy context significantly affected the potential impact of the Children's Fund at this time and damaged the local and national credibility of the initiative (NECF, 2004).

As a preventative programme, the Children's Fund programme sought to drive forward the profile of prevention and preventative services through local multi-agency partnerships, and was in many ways the forerunner of aspects of the 2004 Children Act and its associated guidance. It promoted the participation of children and young people in the design and delivery of services and offered the opportunity for localities to test out partnership working and innovative practices.

The programme funded a range of enhanced and/or new services that addressed risk and protective factors that had been identified in the pre-funding mapping undertaken by each partnership (CYPU, 2001b). The added emphasis on youth justice that occurred part way into the life of the Children's Fund gave troubled and troublesome young people a raised profile within the initiative for a period of time. It is therefore useful to consider the overall context for this aspect of the work of the Children's Fund.

Youth justice

At the same time as the policy relating to child welfare and prevention was undergoing significant change, there were also changes taking place in the way in which youth justice was being addressed. Although it is not the focus of this book, developments in youth justice policy and practice relate to and influence approaches to child welfare and current understandings of prevention in particular. We do not, indeed cannot, present a full history of this area, which is long and complex; there is a rich and broad literature where this is described, debated and analysed within its own disciplinary frameworks (see, for example, Muncie et al, 2002; Smith, 2003; and Tilley, 2005, for introductions to the discipline). Yet this is also why youth justice merits some consideration here – while understandings from youth justice have become increasingly influential on support services for children, young people and families, it is important to recognise that youth justice has its own particular history, one that has not always been in tandem with child and family services in the way that it currently appears to be.

The establishment of a new youth justice system was an immediate priority for the New Labour government on coming to power in 1997, following a damning report from the Audit Commission in 1996 that identified the system as inefficient and failing (Pitts, 2001). The 1998 Crime and Disorder Act established the foundations of a new youth justice system, with the Youth Justice Board established at the centre of a network of local Youth Offending Teams in each local authority and tasked with overseeing and delivering both sanctions and preventative measures within a framework of defined performance management targets. While the related approach to youth crime can be characterised as increasingly punitive, with increases in sentencing and a reduction in the age of criminal responsibility to 10 years of age (for example, Ryan, 2005; Goldson and Muncie, 2006), there has also been evidence of an increasingly preventative and arguably welfare-oriented approach (Burnett and Appleton, 2004; Hughes et al, 2007).

This approach recognises that there are issues within young people's lives that influence their behaviours and that, by addressing interrelated needs in a holistic way, offending behaviour can be reduced (Mason and Prior, 2008). Nonetheless, this aspect sometimes sits uncomfortably within a more punitive discourse that emphasises the need to punish offenders and those families that are at high risk of involvement in crime and antisocial behaviour.

Tensions between welfare and punitive approaches have been a consistent feature of youth justice policy and practice. While youth have consistently been identified as a social problem throughout modernity (France, 2008), approaches to the problem of youth crime have moved between welfare and punitive frameworks. In the 1960s, a welfare approach was reflected in the 1969 Children and Young Persons Act, which saw young people who offend as young people in need of care and protection. The 1970s saw a move away from this approach, instigated by the Conservative government, which amended the provisions of the 1969 Act to introduce a greater emphasis on punishment. This culminated in the 1982 Criminal Justice Act. This Act introduced greater sentencing powers, reflecting an increasing focus on individual and parental responsibility. During the Thatcher government, contrary to popular understanding, policy began to move away from a punishment-centred approach to one that saw prison as ineffective, and promoted community and other sanctions as being more effective to deterrence. While not a purely welfare approach, political pressures and a new Home Secretary in Michael Howard steered policy back towards a punishment-centred approach before such measures could take hold. In 1994, 'Boot Camps' were proposed for young offenders, despite the evidence that the 'short, sharp, shock' regimes of the early 1980s had failed. Thus, the election campaign leading up to the 1997 General Election became dominated by debates over which political party was the toughest on crime and offenders and the true party of law and order (a perennial election issue) (MacMillan and Brown, 1998; Ryan, 2005).

As described earlier in the context of national preventative programmes, New Labour's commitment to 'evidence-based policy' (Coote et al, 2004) and to an associated reinvigoration of policy, including youth justice, coincided with the emergence of 'risk and protective factors' as an increasingly dominant feature of the search within youth and criminal justice for evidence of 'what works'. The 1970s had seen the emergence of 'nothing works', as evidence from interventions in the US and UK and meta-analyses of these failed to establish evidence of effective practice (McGuire, 2002). The dominant tradition of criminology has links with developmental psychology and the sociology of deviance that is positivist in nature; it seeks to establish the facts of offending and non-offending and the characteristics that determine this (France, 2008). Longitudinal research undertaken within this paradigm by Farrington and colleagues (for example, West and Farrington, 1977; Farrington 1996) as 'the Cambridge study' (research following a cohort of 440 males, beginning in the 1950s, in an area of London) established the links between particular risk factors and clusters of them in predicting offending in later life. Despite criticisms of the paradigm, for example as being rooted in a particular time and place (for instance, both communities and crimes have changed since the cohort were in their youth and younger years), this apparent ability to predict offending has been particularly influential, presenting policy makers with a 'prevention science' on which to base policy and practice (Pitts, 2001; France, 2008).

As we have argued earlier, the risk and protective factors framework has focused on 'risk' much more than 'protection', with the interplay between the two little understood beyond the identification of protective factors as the converse of risk (France and Utting, 2005). While we highlight its influence in the thinking about prevention within the Children's Fund in our discussion in Chapter Five, it is necessary to recognise that the framework is rooted in an approach to preventing crime among young people (and stems from a particular approach to quantitative, measurable evidence rooted in the history of criminology and youth studies). From a concern with targeting those at risk of involvement in crime in order to prevent offending, has developed a broader conception of children and young people 'at risk of social exclusion' where crime is one of many interrelated dimensions. Thus, the holistic approaches suggested by the Youth Justice Board are based within an understanding of risk and protective factors that informs all policy and practice, from assessment and the tools that Youth Offending Teams and practitioners are required to use, to the interventions that stem from this assessment and which aim to address risk and increase protective factors (YJB, 2005). The influence of the framework became explicit with the announcement of 'the 25%' and the associated menu of options from which Children's Fund partnerships were required to select. The links between crime prevention and social exclusion more broadly were complete.

In fact, this merging of crime and social exclusion could be seen in the development of policy as the Children's Fund emerged as an initiative. On Track was established by the Home Office in 1999 and sought to pilot preventative services for children involved in, and at risk of involvement in, crime and antisocial behaviour. Twenty-four neighbourhood-level programmes in England and Wales targeted 4- to 12-year-olds through an interrelated set of five targeted interventions (to be experienced by users as 'multiple interventions'). Before the piloting of interventions could be completed, or even firmly established, the initiative was transferred to the CYPU and On Track programmes were merged with local Children's Funds. Connections between the two were diverse and complex, with some local areas protecting On Track programmes as separate elements of activity and some building on or extending interventions to other groups (NECF, 2003a). This merging had two features we can reflect on here. First, the piloting intended could not be completed and thus the testing of multiple interventions was never realised; early evaluation reports focused on implementation, and later evaluation findings (relating to impact) were not published. The evaluations of both On Track and the Children's Fund reported on the operational difficulties for both the programmes and their evaluations in achieving implementation as designed and thus demonstrating impacts. But second, the shift of this Home Office crime reduction initiative into the broader CYPU and Children's Fund programme illustrated the bringing together of this more focused crime agenda with a focus on social exclusion where risk of involvement in crime is one, key, feature.

Conclusion

Political interpretations of prevention, risk and social exclusion can be seen to have been key drivers in New Labour's development of preventative child welfare provision. The policy backdrop has changed dramatically from the early, inherited one of individualised assessment of childhood risk and need, to a much broader aspiration of avoiding the harms that result from socially exclusionary processes that affect many children who live in poor neighbourhoods, or who are members of social groups most at risk of exclusion regardless of where they live. However, while this more structural analysis of the difficulties faced by some children and their families might suggest a radical approach to ensuring welfare and well-being, the notion of 'preventing social exclusion' became somewhat diluted so that 'prevention' became interpreted as meaning avoiding the need for more intensive modes of intervention.

Preventative policies relating specifically to children (and sometimes their families) were implemented alongside other initiatives designed to address the need to 'regenerate' (and later 'empower') disadvantaged communities, and to address specific inequalities such as health and educational achievement. But the learning opportunities across and between the national initiatives were often not taken forward – leading to isolated strands of activity that struggled to 'join up' to address the broad change agenda. In Chapters Five and Six we discuss how this political framing of prevention as a process of reducing potential later acute difficulties and poor outcomes was interpreted and applied in some Children's Fund partnerships. Chapter Five begins this analysis by considering the strategies adopted by partnerships seeking to reduce negative consequences of social exclusion.

FIVE

The Children's Fund: strategies for social inclusion

Introduction

The Guidance issued by the Children and Young People's Unit (CYPU) to partnerships established to deliver the Children's Fund objectives (CYPU, 2001b) directed attention to 'those children, young people and families most at risk of social exclusion through poverty and disadvantage', providing 'joined-up support' to address 'often multifaceted problems'. It was up to local Children's Fund partnerships to determine which children and families in their areas should be targeted (Hughes and Fielding, 2006), but the assumption underpinning the initiative that was implemented in every local authority in England was that the risk of social exclusion was not one that was restricted to areas of the country recognised to be particularly disadvantaged. Unlike the New Deal for Communities, Health Action Zones and other 'area-based initiatives' introduced by New Labour to address problems of disadvantage and social exclusion in those areas most adversely affected by inequalities, the Children's Fund was universal to the extent that all local authorities were required to put programmes in place in collaboration with other statutory and voluntary sector partners. However, partnerships were expected to 'target' their activities within the local area and this implied the capacity both to determine how and where activities should be targeted and to develop appropriate strategies for responding to the issues and needs identified in the process of targeting. In this chapter we consider how Children's Fund partnerships went about determining how to focus their activities and the nature of the strategies they adopted for work with some of the most marginalised groups of children and young people.

Targeting for prevention

In Chapter Three we discussed the impact of the risk and protection discourses in shaping the thinking behind the Children's Fund and other policy initiatives focused on children and young people. In

Chapter Four we considered the relationship between the way in which notions of prevention are being used in these contexts and how this relates to conceptualisations of social exclusion. We highlighted the way in which a 'tiered' approach to prevention can lead to policies variously intended to be focused at the 'top' or 'bottom' ends of the risk spectrum. Schoon and Bynner (2003) suggest that research that explores risk, protection and resilience has a number of implications for social policy. The emphasis on primary prevention rather than crisis intervention after harm has been caused requires the ability to identify those who may be harmed, but who are not already exhibiting signs of this. Similar approaches are evident in the context of initiatives to 'case find' older people 'at risk' of admission to hospital who can then be targeted by prevention programmes (Billings et al, 2006; King's Fund, 2006), and in relation to initiatives to target 'disadvantaged mothers' during pregnancy in order to deliver intensive support until their child is two years old (Olds, 2006).

Schoon and Bynner (2003) argue that while certain groups may be identified as 'vulnerable', they may still have strengths that can be utilised to achieve change. Together with the need to ensure that strategies for prevention are culturally sensitive and appropriate, and actively engage with the child or young person, this implies an approach that recognises the personal and collective agency of children who belong to social groups considered to be 'vulnerable' to social exclusion. We highlighted a similar issue when considering the role of 'resistance' as a strategy adopted by marginalised groups who may be excluded from mainstream society but who develop their own sources of support and who are actively engaged within their own communities (Chapter Two). Schoon and Bynner also highlight the importance of approaches that are holistic, that integrate service delivery and involve families and communities in addition to the young people themselves. They also note that 'vulnerability' is circumstantial: children have different 'sensitive periods' during their development and may be in or out of risk at various points in their lives due to changing circumstances.

If we add to these observations the recognition that children and young people are excluded by attitudes, policies and processes to which they are subject, but over which they have little if any control (Chapter Two), then this implies that strategies based solely on identifying individuals or groups of children as 'the problem' to be targeted, will have limited success. However, recent policy developments such as Sure Start and On Track have drawn on a growing range of longitudinal survey data and quantitative approaches to identify risk and protective factors that influence children and young people's chances of negative outcomes in later life and have used this to determine which children should be targeted for intervention (see, for example, Benard, 1991; Newman, 2002; Schoon and Bynner, 2003). Such research has identified factors related to the characteristics and attributes of individual children, families, peer groups, schools and communities that contribute to poor outcomes and this has been highly influential in the design of interventions intended to avert certain outcomes, particularly in relation to crime and antisocial behaviour (Prior and Paris, 2005). However, most such interventions are designed to address individual and family circumstances rather than the broader social contexts that contribute to negative outcomes. The development of strategies has thus not been able to respond fully in order to counteract the range of identified risk indicators.

There are many reasons for this. One is that the challenge of identifying and thus targeting *individuals* on the basis of research evidence about their likely risk profile is substantial. Feinstein and Sabates (2006) highlighted the significance of the availability of full information in applying UK Birth Cohort data to predicting which children would evidence 'high cost or high harm' outcomes as adults. With full information about children at age 11, 70.8% of cases of multiple deprivation at age 23 was predicted, with only 1.4% falsely predicted (that is, they did not end up experiencing the expected level of deprivation). When full information was not available, the false positives increased to 5.2% and only 41.1% of cases of multiple deprivation was predicted. Such approaches are thus highly dependent on the availability and accuracy of data sources and even comprehensive information will not identify all those likely to be affected. But the identification of individuals, groups or areas at risk of social exclusion is also largely dependent on which indicators are chosen to generate composite deprivation 'scores' (see Percy-Smith, 2000, p 8). This approach, which is used in a range of circumstances in which actuarial calculations are made to assess insurance risks, cannot absolutely predict which individuals will become subject to the risk being assessed. Any variation in the combination or weighting of indicators will produce different outcomes suggesting a different focus for intervention, and the choice of indicators to be used to identify the likelihood of exclusion is disputed. For example, living in single-parent households is often used as an indicator of potential disadvantage, but not all such children are disadvantaged.

Assuming that some consensus *can* be reached about appropriate indicators to include, the technical task of utilising such data to calculate overall risk factors is a complex one (Hansen and Plewis, 2004). Risk factors have a cumulative negative effect on children and young people's lives, but research on risk has tended to be based on simplified numerical calculations that do not deal with the way in which risk factors interact with each other, nor with issues of process or context (France and Utting, 2005). In addition, policy makers and implementers have to make use of what data is kept, usually for administrative purposes, rather than collecting data that is directly relevant to the issue or objective that is the focus for action. Thus, for example, much of the existing data relating to the circumstances of children and young people that those planning the Children's Fund might have made use of was not appropriate because it did not relate to the focus on prevention (NECF, 2004). Data on 'looked-after' children, for example, identify those for whom much preventative activity would come too late to prevent family breakdown and the likely consequences of this. Relying on data collected for other purposes in order to develop proxies for identifying risk among populations can result in doubtful assumptions being made. Often, geographical areas (usually as large as a ward) or identifiable target groups are used as proxies for risk. This leads to an area-based definition of risk, but this does not mean that all children living in these areas are at risk and nor does this identify children outside these areas who may be disadvantaged (Hansen and Plewis, 2004).

Even if these technical problems were to be overcome, this does not address the dynamic processes of exclusion and the issue of identifying and targeting factors that contribute to this. In the early days of the disability movement, Michael Oliver, a disability activist and academic, challenged the effort being put into creating registers of disabled people as a basis on which to design services. Rather than counting disabled people, he argued, effort should be spent in identifying disabling aspects of the environment and targeting them for action. This highlights the question not only of who or what should be targeted, but of who should define the terms within which those 'at risk' might be identified – should it be policy makers, statistical experts or those who are themselves likely to be included as 'targets'?

In this context, analysis of the approaches used by Children's Fund partnerships to targeting their activities revealed a combination of evidence-based, professionally inspired and user-informed decision-making processes (Hughes and Fielding, 2006). Quantitative data were used to identify areas experiencing broadly defined deprivation, more specific aspects of needs within areas or needs of particular groups (such as black and minority ethnic children) within areas. Data sources varied between local authorities but there were widespread concerns about the value of existing data for the purpose of Children's Fund targeting, a recognition that data were patchy in coverage (for example, an absence of area-based data about groups such as young carers, children whose parents experience mental health problems, or Travellers) and some evidence of inadequate skills to conduct the necessary analysis.

Guidance required partnerships to involve children, young people and their parents within the Children's Fund and consultations with actual and potential users were used to inform targeting decisions in a number of ways. Some authorities used consultation to inform initial decisions about areas, groups or models to be targeted while others took these initial decisions and then sought input from children and families in order to gain a greater understanding of the needs and circumstances to which they should be responding. In other cases, user input came at the point at which services were being commissioned to respond to needs (see below).

The views and knowledge of service providers were seen as a means of augmenting the lack of evaluative data that would assist in determining the likely effectiveness of service models, and the lack of data describing the needs of particular groups, such as the needs of new refugees and asylum seekers. On occasion, provider input was sought in order to make the earliest decisions concerning groups or areas to be targeted and time constraints sometimes led to a reliance on this source of data rather than the collection of primary data. But more usually, such input came after the identification of priority groups in order to build up a more detailed understanding.

Where it existed, partnerships drew on research evidence in similar ways to their consultations with service providers. The main body of research evidence that informed such decisions related to risk and protective factors relating to youth crime, although research evidence was also cited more generally as a basis for labelling certain groups as 'vulnerable'. Evaluation evidence was used to support particular models of practice and in some areas a requirement to provide research evidence to justify proposals formed part of the commissioning process. Local mapping of existing provision and gaps within this also informed decisions.

These different sources of data and insight resulted in the identification of particular areas within the local authority on which to focus activity, and, closely related to this, the identification of schools within which to base services (sometimes because it was pupils in a particular school who were being targeted and sometimes because a school was a convenient location for services intended to be accessible to other children living in the area). Specific groups of children were also identified as targets for action, regardless of where they lived. These included social groups such as minority ethnic children and Gypsy/Traveller children; children in particular circumstances, such as those caring for a disabled relative; and children defined by actual or potential behaviours, primarily those considered to be likely to commit crimes or become involved in antisocial behaviour. In addition, there were some instances where individual children were identified, for example via 'Children's Fund Champions' or by locating services in sites such as schools, community centres or childcare settings that were most often used by individuals who might be targets. Another targeting strategy developed out of a commitment to a particular model or way of working. For example, play provision and an application of family support models were considered means of addressing multiple needs and circumstances and thus were applied in different geographical areas and in order to respond to the needs of different groups. Play services, for example, served different ends depending on whether they were targeted at disabled children or children at risk of antisocial behaviour.

The targeting decisions made by individual partnerships indicate how they were both defining and identifying children at risk of social exclusion. The definitions of groups to be targeted revealed the complexity and contestability of this process. In some cases, official, standardised definitions are available and were adopted in order to identify need. For example, some partnerships used the Disability Register to identify disabled children, and some drew on legal definitions of refugee or asylum-seeker status in order to define children considered to be at risk of exclusion. However, such administrative and legal categories do not resolve the issue of definition, nor that of identifying common or shared needs. In addition to the use of social group categories, group or thematic targeting also sought to identify children and young people by reference to experiential or behavioural classifications: bullying, antisocial behaviour or other behavioural difficulties, for example. Such categories raised further definitional difficulties (Prior et al, 2006).

Defining target groups

We can illustrate some of these definitional issues faced by partnerships by considering ways in which selected partnerships approached the four groups selected for detailed study by the national evaluation of the Children's Fund.

Disabled children

While we, as evaluators, used the language of 'disabled children' because we were influenced by the social model of disability and the perspective this offers on those factors that prevent disabled children from taking part in activities alongside their non-disabled peers (see Clarke, 2006), Children's Fund partnerships more often used the language of 'special needs' – reflecting the dominance of educational rather than social welfare discourses – to describe one group targeted for action by 88% of partnerships (Edwards et al, 2006, chapter 6). In one partnership, service providers used the terms 'disabled children', 'children with disabilities' and 'children with special needs' almost interchangeably. Children using the services commissioned by the Children's Fund had learning difficulties, communication difficulties, sensory impairments or diagnoses such as autism, Aspergers or attention deficit hyperactivity disorder (ADHD). Some had physical impairments but only a minority had more complex needs requiring high levels of support. Funding decisions indicated that the concept of 'special needs' was not considered to include children at risk of developing mental health problems (Barnes et al, 2006a).

There was evidence of difference over language: some people thought that the term 'special needs' was helpful in emphasising the additional support children needed, rather than labelling them with particular diagnoses, while others felt that the term was unhelpfully non-specific. The terms 'inclusion' and 'integration' also highlighted different assumptions about objectives and this interacted with the way in which different people interpreted who could be targeted within the terms of reference of the Children's Fund. From one perspective, children with severe impairments or complex healthcare needs were excluded because they were in receipt of and continued to need specialist services and it was not possible to intervene at the 'low end' of the prevention spectrum. As well as reinforcing our concern about the unsatisfactory nature of the 'levels' analysis of prevention (Morris and Barnes, 2008), this indicates how policies ostensibly intended to prevent exclusion could result in further marginalisation. From another perspective, some parents felt that their children were not regarded as having a sufficiently high level of need to enable them to receive a service.

Black and minority ethnic children

Following Ahmed (2004), the National Evaluation of the Children's Fund (NECF) used the term 'black and minority ethnic' children to refer to 'people of African, Caribbean and South Asian descent. This term also includes people of Chinese origins and people of mixed race who have one parent from these groups' (Ahmed, 2004, p 3). However, Ahmed notes that the use of the term 'black' to include South Asian groups has been contested, and that socioeconomic, cultural, religious and other differences within and between minority ethnic groups mean that the political strategy associated with the use of the term 'black' may no longer be acceptable. The two partnerships we looked at in this context adopted a rather different approach to defining this target group. In one city there was an above-average and varied black and minority ethnic population and the partnership's focus was solely on African Caribbean children (and originally only African Caribbean boys). In the other city the focus was broader and included children from African Caribbean, Asian and mixed heritage backgrounds. This city also has a diverse population, with a proportion of children from black and minority ethnic groups equal to the UK average. In both cases it was concerns about educational attendance and attainment, high rates of school exclusion among African Caribbean boys and the overrepresentation of African Caribbean children in the local looked-after children population that resulted in the identification of specific ethnic groups as targets for action (Morris et al, 2006).

Gypsies/Travellers

The term 'Gypsy/Traveller' includes different cultural groups including Roma, Irish Travellers, fairground people and New Age Travellers. But in this instance it was the broad cultural characteristic of a travelling lifestyle and the consequences of this that led to the targeting of this group, and to the decision that it made sense to work collaboratively across a number of partnerships to develop a response. This decision was also influenced by the existence of a regional Traveller education service, which not only offered something of a model for a service response that reflected at least one aspect of the culture of the group concerned, it also influenced the way in which the needs of the group were defined for the purposes of the Children's Fund. In this instance, it was not education, but access to leisure services that was the focus in order to address a perceived gap in services. However, in practice, many of those who used the services provided by the consortium of partnerships we studied were less mobile than others and some were housed. The key criterion appeared to be that families were prepared to make use of the service, rather than the group being defined more precisely by service providers (Mason et al, 2006).

Refugees and asylum-seeking children

In the case of refugee and asylum-seeking children, we saw important distinctions in the approach to definition (while recognising that within this group, refugee children and asylum-seeking children have a different legal status and different rights). In the two partnerships we looked at the decision to target refugees and asylum seekers was taken within a context in which local demography was undergoing significant changes due to a rise in the number of newly arrived people from a wide range of countries. Mainstream services and agencies were experiencing difficulties in reaching this target group and fulfilling their statutory obligations of responding to their needs and interests. Particular issues and concerns were coming to the fore in schools and political interest was creating a momentum for action. Neither partnership used legal definitions as the basis for determining precisely who should be targeted, but each reached different conclusions about which groups should be targeted on the basis of need, the specific objectives of the organisations and projects funded and the interests of stakeholders involved. In one partnership this resulted in a focus on newly arrived children and their families and the multiple factors that constrain their integration and settlement into their new school, in particular, and their new environment, in general. The other partnership worked with both newly arrived children and young people and second-generation refugees. This decision resulted from the growing concerns within the education service about the underachievement of this group. Such concerns were shared by representatives of the more established second-generation refugee communities. The two partnerships did not target unaccompanied asylum seekers. These are children who arrive as asylum seekers without adults, with associated legal frameworks, and were judged in both partnerships to require more acute support than the early intervention preventative aims of the Children's Fund were seen to allow.

These differences suggest that the first partnership constructed its target group around the experiences of newly arrived people, with a particular focus on those who had endured traumatic events, while the second partnership reflected a concern with how the experiences of being a refugee or asylum seeker and a member of a particular ethnic group affected young people's chances of social inclusion (Beirens et al, 2006).

In each of these cases there was strong input from providers in determining the precise definition of the target group and the particular needs and issues to which the Children's Fund should respond. This approach was rather different from the way in which Children's Fund partnerships, for example, identified children and young people on whom to target actions intended to prevent or reduce crime and antisocial behaviour. In this case they adopted definitions of the target group based in assumptions about the kinds of children likely to become engaged in criminal or antisocial activities, which themselves derive from a substantial body of, primarily, quantitative research (Mason and Prior, 2008).

Commissioning for prevention

Having taken decisions to target specific groups or areas, Children's Fund partnerships then had to decide what types of services or activities to put in place in order to respond to the risk of social exclusion faced by these children and young people. Experience of other complex community initiatives with broad social change objectives indicates that those responsible for developing and delivering programmes may be better at identifying the problems than they are at determining what the appropriate responses are (Connell and Kubisch, 1998). One factor that contributed to the growth of interest in theories of change as an approach to the evaluation of complex community initiatives was the recognition that decisions about what to do and why in such contexts were often not well thought through. In particular, those charged with implementing such policy initiatives were often not able to specify *why* the activities they were proposing were anticipated to deliver their desired outcomes. Theories-of-change evaluation was designed to contribute a developmental as well as an evaluative input in this context and the 'ideal' context for theories-of-change evaluation has been argued to be where the researchers are able to work with stakeholders in the process of programme planning and then follow through implementation to assess the robustness of the theory in use that underlies the programme design. One of the overall conclusions from the national evaluation of Health Action Zones (which utilised a theories-of-change approach but was unable to start the process at programme design stage) was that there was not a strong relationship between the activities put in place and the outcome objectives they were intended to achieve (Barnes et al, 2005). So, were the targeting decisions made by Children's Fund partnerships translated into activities informed by robust decisions about why and how these would respond to the identified problems and deliver the intended outcomes?

Partnerships adopted a variety of approaches to commissioning services, which themselves reflected different assumptions about how to ensure that activities would deliver intended outcomes (Hughes and Fielding, 2006). The first approach identified – commissioning against predefined models – was based on the partnership board predefining the model or way of working that it considered most likely to be appropriate and inviting tenders to deliver this service. Sometimes this was based on evidence of effective practice, in other cases it was more a question of filling perceived gaps in service provision, extending existing provision to new areas or delivering on what the partnership had identified as its priorities. In cases where there was agreement about the needs and risks to be addressed, but little or no preconceived ideas about how they might be addressed, partnerships invited tenders against identified needs and those groups doing the commissioning were required to evidence the rationale for their decisions – the second approach. In some cases the partnership produced a template designed to facilitate this process. The third approach represented a rather greater degree of devolution of responsibility. Here, commissioning groups relating to areas or thematic groups had responsibility for commissioning decisions on the basis that they were considered to be closest to, and have the best understanding of, the needs to be addressed. And fourth, some partnerships adopted an open bidding approach to commissioning, aiming to attract as many proposals as possible against a very loose set of criteria. One partnership that adopted this approach employed staff to work with those agencies who wanted to bid to help them develop proposals that would meet Children's Fund criteria while also aiming to stimulate innovation. This approach is reminiscent of the 'developmental commissioning' approach developed in other initiatives (for example Lambeth, Lewisham and Southwark Health Action Zone), which was intended to enable small voluntary organisations, particularly those working with minority ethnic communities, to make a contribution to the overall programme (Barnes et al, 2001).

These different approaches to commissioning can be summarised as:

- 'the partnership knows best';
- 'we know what we want but we don't know how to get there';
- 'specialist groups are best placed to come up with the right proposals'; and finally
- 'let a thousand flowers bloom'.

Evaluation evidence suggests that partnerships learnt how to do commissioning over time and evidence from the Health Action Zone evaluation also demonstrates the way in which strategies for collaboration evolved in response to changing circumstances and the learning that took place within partnerships (Barnes et al, 2003). We do not have evidence that might suggest which is the 'best' approach to either targeting or commissioning and experience suggests that different approaches may be adopted within the same partnership for different purposes and at different times. In complex open systems there will always be unintended consequences of whatever approach is adopted and prediction in the context of service systems is as uncertain as it is in the context of outcomes for children and young people (Haynes, 2003).

While it may be wholly unrealistic and overly conservative to expect approaches to service commissioning based solely on evidence about the likely effectiveness of interventions, the analysis of social exclusion presented in Chapter Two does suggest that effective programmes will be those that are capable of responding to the range of factors that constitute the experience of exclusion and which tackle the factors that exclude as well as focusing on the children and young people who may be excluded. This implies that whatever approach to commissioning is employed, there is a need to consider not only what contribution individual services can make, but also how services collectively might comprise a coherent programme in respect to the overall objectives. It also implies that some activities may not be focused directly on the children themselves, but on the barriers they face. And, acknowledging the specific CYPU (2001b) Guidance on this as well as taking a realistic perspective on what it is possible for any special initiative to achieve (however well resourced), there is also a need to consider how partnerships might 'bend the mainstream' and otherwise act to help deliver objectives other than via commissioning time-limited services.

Spelling out the strategies

We can consider these issues in more detail by looking at how selected Children's Fund partnerships approached the development of programmes focused on groups of children and young people who are among those most at risk of social exclusion. We studied work with disabled children, black and minority ethnic children and children who are refugees, each in two different partnerships, making a total of six thematic case studies. The work with Gypsy/Traveller children was slightly different – here we worked with a regional consortium involving six partnerships when our work commenced, who sought to come together to develop their services for this group of children and families.

A survey conducted in autumn 2005 of Children's Fund programme managers (Edwards et al, 2006) indicated the ongoing targeting of, and therefore the recognition of, the persistent need to provide support for the groups at the centre of the research:

- 88.3% of partnerships targeted disabled children;
- 70.8% of partnerships targeted black and minority ethnic children;
- 47.5% of partnerships targeted Gypsy/Traveller children;
- 43.3% of partnerships targeted refugee and asylum-seeking children.

The descriptions of the strategies described here are the result of a co-construction involving researchers as well as the stakeholders directly responsible for the development of the strategies in the context of a theories-of-change evaluation (Mason and Barnes, 2007). The theory-of-change narratives suggest how each of these partnerships understood the risks of social exclusion faced by the different groups of children and how these might be prevented. This also relates to the way in which such groups were defined. Here we summarise key aspects of each partnership's approach from this perspective. We describe the activities and services that resulted from such decisions, and their impact, in Chapter Six.

Disabled children

One partnership targeting disabled children expressed outcomes for children in terms of improved emotional health and well-being; enhanced life and independence skills; and the maximisation of their potential. Recognising the impact of disability on the family as a whole, it also defined outcome objectives in terms of improved family relationships and preventing family breakdown. In addition, the partnership defined service objectives that would be a necessary contribution to the achievement of these objectives. These centred around increasing awareness, capacity and skills within and across mainstream agencies in working with disabled children, working towards a sustainable service that would prevent the need for more intensive interventions and increased access.

The way in which the child outcome objectives were defined reflects the individualised perspective on social exclusion that dominated the overall objectives of the Children's Fund. Rather than focusing on removing the barriers to inclusion for disabled children, the emphasis was on improving individual capacities to resist such impediments. Thus, there was considerable emphasis on the need to increase confidence in their own abilities, develop their own interests, improve family relationships and give disabled children experiences that would make them happier.

While the second partnership defined outcomes rather differently, the focus was still on individual disabled children. Here the emphasis was on increasing children's participation in services; increasing their confidence; enabling them to gain qualifications that would in turn increase their employment possibilities; and encouraging some children who had been users of services to become involved in running them. Service objectives focused on the creation of a comprehensive and integrated range of services, in which parents and children had a strong voice. They aimed to improve both accessibility and sustainability of services. The emphasis on voice and participation reflected the less-developed nature of parental involvement in this partnership in comparison with the other partnership. Such involvement was seen as a way of ensuring a higher profile for services for disabled children and that children would remain with the services and develop skills to organise their own activities. Services for the whole family were also considered to lessen the likelihood that siblings would feel left out, to help parents recognise their children's capabilities, to reduce the strain of caring for a disabled child and to improve the quality of family relationships. In some parts of the local authority area, the intention was to make services available to all children in order to make it easier for friendships to develop and to encourage moves towards integration. It was also hoped that children would be introduced to other activities relevant to their interests through the contacts service providers had with other services.

Black and minority ethnic children

Although, as we have seen, this target group was defined rather differently in the two partnerships we looked at, both defined similar outcome objectives and suggested similar rationales for the activities they put in place. Outcome objectives emphasised the need to respond to evidence of poor educational outcomes in comparison with the white population. Providing additional learning opportunities based outside traditional school settings and located within children's communities was seen as a way of improving formal educational attainments. Enabling new experiences for black and minority ethnic children that engaged them positively in learning and education was also seen as a way to help them cope better within formal educational settings; and providing support for children's networks in helping children navigate the formal education system was also considered a way of assisting them to achieve better outcomes. In both partnerships, strategies aimed to build on and support community-based provision to ensure that the services accurately reflected the needs, heritage and experiences of black and minority ethnic children and offered disadvantaged families support and practical help. It was considered important to balance the negative or absent mainstream black and minority ethnic images with positive cultural images and experiences to enable children to grow in confidence and assist them in coping with racism and oppression.

Partnerships also recognised the need to change existing practices in order to achieve better services for black and minority ethnic children. The decision to target this group reflected evidence of a failure of existing mainstream provision to meet needs, and thus the necessity to develop specially targeted services. This was reflected in the structures developed by the two partnerships: both rolled out service development under the umbrella of a specific black and minority ethnic task or reference group and emphasised the role to be played by providers within children's communities to meet needs and support links into the mainstream. In both partnerships, supporting local community-based providers was presented as an opportunity to build on existing strengths and expertise, and to ensure that services adequately reflected children's needs and life experiences.

Gypsy/Traveller children

The decision to establish a regional consortium as a basis from which to commission services for Gypsy/Traveller children was intended to reflect the movement of families across local authority boundaries. Thus, the fundamental design characteristic was a positive expression of the importance of working with the culture of this group, rather than expecting them to adjust to the assumptions of the settled community. The creation of this consortium also reflected a number of other assumptions, including the need for a critical mass of partnerships to be involved to make this work viable, the need to respond to different characteristics of the areas within the consortium and the importance of leadership and support from the Government Office of the Region.

The strategy of the consortium had four strands. First, it recognised the need to work with mainstream service providers and workers delivering other Children's Fund services in order to raise awareness, develop more appropriate services sensitive to Gypsy/Traveller needs and ensure a greater consistency of services across the region. It was argued that Gypsy/Traveller children and families would be more likely to make use of such services and would not experience disadvantage in service use because of their mobility.

Second, it was considered important to work with parents in order to build awareness of available services, to develop confidence and self-esteem and to ensure that they knew they had rights to services. The importance of this was related to a perceived reticence in using services not traditionally valued in Gypsy/Traveller culture, and fears that if children take part in mainstream services this would lead to what some described as culture loss.

Third, the main focus of the strategy was based around the belief that providing direct support to enable children to access play and leisure services would build their confidence and self-esteem. It was suggested that positive experiences would encourage Gypsy/Traveller children to seek out other opportunities without direct support. This in turn would improve well-being and lead to improved outcomes.

Finally, the theory of change also recognised the importance of educating the settled community in order to raise awareness and reduce discrimination. However, those planning this initiative thought that there were limited resources to allocate to this aspect of the strategy and any impact in this respect would primarily be a side-effect of work with service providers.

Overall, the approach assumed that increased use of mainstream services rather than the development of new services based around Gypsy/Traveller lifestyles and culture was the main route by which the social inclusion of Gypsy/Traveller children would be achieved.

Refugee and asylum-seeking children

Education and emotional well-being were viewed as key to achieving the social inclusion of young refugees and asylum seekers. Both partnerships studied by NECF aimed to ensure that schools provided places for newly arrived children, offered appropriate induction, acknowledged the skills and knowledge children have prior to arrival and helped them to realise their full potential. Both partnerships assumed that developing home–school liaison would not only enhance educational attendance and attainment of individual children, but also contribute to schools' understanding of the needs, concerns and interests of refugees or asylum-seeking children. The difference, as we have seen, is that one partnership aimed to provide packages of support responsive to the immediate needs of newly arrived children and their families. It adopted a strengths-based model that aimed to mobilise the capacities of refugee and asylum-seeking parents and families. The other also focused on educational support, but also took action to promote the cultural identity of more established refugee communities. It thus had more of an emphasis on improving community cohesion and integration, drawing on the knowledge, skills and resources of reasonably well-established voluntary or community-based organisations.

Enabling educational attendance and attainment was seen to necessitate attention to the emotional well-being of refugee and asylum-seeking children and this led to a decision to fund therapeutic services for children suffering emotional problems. Promoting children's emotional and social skills was seen as a way not only of enabling children to deal with the difficult experiences they had gone through but also of helping children to make new friends and facilitate integration within their new environments. One partnership supported therapeutic services for the family as a whole, reflecting the view that changing the social environment of the child was essential to the pursuit of emotional well-being and social inclusion.

The long-term objectives of the two programmes also focused on raising capacity within organisations and changing practice, including the mainstreaming of therapeutic interventions. They aimed to facilitate links and share information, act as advocates, organise awareness-raising events, deliver training packages and pilot new measures, activities and initiatives.

In different ways, both these partnerships demonstrated a more holistic response to the dimensions of exclusion in this context than was evident in strategies in relation to the other three groups. Perhaps because targeting refugees and asylum seekers was a comparatively new policy objective, it appeared to be possible not only to respond to individual circumstances, but also to work with children in the context of their families and their ethnic or cultural communities. It also appeared to be possible to acknowledge that public services and policies could themselves contribute to exclusion and needed to change, and to offer practical responses to the discrimination that refugees and asylum seekers could experience from 'host' communities, for example, by helping families find accommodation in more supportive localities.

Conclusion

Reviewing the approaches adopted as a whole in the context of the theorisation of prevention and social exclusion and the evidence of the circumstances of particular groups of children set out in Chapter Two, leaves us with a number of questions about the robustness of these strategies.

The whole notion of 'targeting' is contentious. As we have seen, it is both technically and politically complex and highlights the contested nature of both prevention and social exclusion. Because of this, some Children's Fund practitioners expressed concern that targeting specific groups could itself be regarded as exclusionary. But some form of targeting is commonplace even among universal services – health services are primarily targeted at those who are ill, or most likely to become so. The shift to prevention as a guiding principle in social policy will not remove the practical necessity to find some way of defining and identifying those who are a priority for action.

In view of the very different barriers to inclusion faced by the four groups of children we have studied in this analysis, the decision to develop strategies to address these in distinctive ways could be argued to make sense. But what was perhaps more a matter of interest was the limited focus on those barriers in comparison with the aim to build individual resilience to resist their impact. While the theories of change generated with stakeholders demonstrated awareness of the multidimensional nature of social exclusion and in some cases included a specific recognition of the significance of addressing the 'excluders' as well as the 'excluded', this did not always result in a programme of activities capable of responding to these processes. This raises questions about the sustainability of benefits that were experienced and the capacity of these strategies to benefit children in similar circumstances but who are not direct users of services. In the next chapter we look at the way in which these strategies were implemented and at the evidence of the impact they had on children, families and levels of need.

SIX

The Children's Fund: activities and impacts of the partnership strategies

Introduction

In Chapter Five we saw how partnerships targeted different groups for preventative services and action. Target groups may have had the same labels, but how they were defined and the needs that were identified were varied. The lack of centralised prescription as to how preventative strategies might be designed created a situation in which each Children's Fund partnership could invent its own approach. Local targeting required locally appropriate strategies and thus local context was key to the way in which strengths, needs and opportunities were identified and activities and services were commissioned. Potentially, this enabled innovation and experimentation both in creating new services capable of realising the preventative aspirations of the Children's Fund and in 'bending the mainstream' – working with and through statutory service providers to overcome the barriers to refocusing on prevention that was evident following the implementation of the 1989 Children Act.

In this chapter we discuss the activities that were funded, supported and developed by the partnerships that focused on the target groups discussed in Chapter Five. By exploring them more fully, we are able to highlight and discuss the similarities and differences between partnerships in working with the target groups and the impacts that were achieved. We review the way the strategies were implemented and the impacts they had in the short to medium term, and assess the robustness of the approaches adopted in the context of the aims of the Children's Fund. The theories-of-change approach adopted by the evaluation enabled us to explore how local interpretation of national guidance was enacted in practice and thus how preventative policy was implemented.

Disabled children

For our analysis, we looked at a Children's Fund partnership targeting disabled children in a large county authority and one targeting disabled children in a metropolitan authority of three towns. In Chapter Five we saw how different language was used by stakeholders to define this target group and how this interrelated with their strategies. In both partnerships the term 'special needs' was used more frequently than the term 'disabled', and both partnerships adopted a rather loose categorisation of the precise groups that the strategies were targeting.

The large county authority partnership included both geographical target areas and cross-county target groups within its overall strategy. Within its 'Children with Special Needs' programme of activities, it defined the long-term outcome objectives for children and their families as:

- improving emotional health and well-being;
- developing children's life and independence skills;
- maximising children's potential;
- improving family relationships; and (related to this)
- preventing family breakdowns.

It also aimed to achieve a range of changes in existing services for 'children with special needs' and in the related structures and systems. The intended outcomes for services were:

- increased awareness, capacity and skills within mainstream agencies in working with disabled children and children with special needs;
- an appropriate balance of responsibilities and more effective communication between statutory and voluntary agencies; and
- sustainable services that would prevent the need for more intensive interventions and increased access in terms of numbers and geographical equity.

Once 'children with special needs' (termed 'disabled children' from here after) had been identified as a theme for cross-county targeting, existing multi-agency locality groups were involved in agreeing appropriate local and county-wide provision. Parents and carers played an important role in these groups, and a network of parent and carer forums linked to the multi-agency groups provided direct input into these decisions. There were tensions in this approach, with not all groups as well developed as others and differences in the links between the groups and the forums. Some parents and carers were unsure of the impact that their involvement had achieved, while some service providers felt that parent and carer voices had been too powerful. Although there was an uneven focus across the county, a range of services and activities was commissioned and established to achieve the outcome objectives identified. The services supported by the partnership included:

Deaf and Hearing Impaired Children: Support and Advocacy Project. This voluntary sector project was developed from existing provision. A parent-led organisation had provided holiday activities for deaf children. The new project aimed to support and advocate for deaf and hearing impaired children, their families and carers, and promote communication and understanding within mainstream services. Parents and carers were involved in the management of the project and in the delivery of activities. The project delivered a range of services including play and leisure opportunities through holiday activities and after-school clubs. It also encouraged and provided support for parent and carer involvement; provided specialist advice and support, for example within educational provision and structures; and offered sign-language training for all the family. Alongside these child- and family-focused services there were also attempts to target awareness training at mainstream agencies and the project aimed to develop and support multi-agency working through links with mainstream and other voluntary and community sector services.

Special Needs Enabling Services. There were two 'enabling services' commissioned by the partnership. The first was hosted by a Primary Care Trust. The project aimed to provide enabling support for children with special needs to access mainstream play and leisure services independently from their family. The rationale behind this was that these opportunities would enable children to interact positively with their (non-disabled) peers. There was an expectation that, over time, confidence and skills in working with children with special needs would increase among those working in mainstream services, and that this would facilitate the development of enabling provision. The activities that were put in place to achieve this were one-to-one support for six to 12 weeks for disabled children, enabling them to access mainstream play and leisure services, extended enabling support for children with the most complex needs and trips, and, in recognition of the fact that the impact of disability is experienced by other family members, activities for siblings.

The second 'enabling service' was developed in a different locale and was hosted by a private sector organisation with a long history of providing services for disabled people in the area. The service had the same aim as the first, in supporting disabled children and those with a special need to access mainstream services and provision and interact with peers. Although the rationale behind the service was the same as in the first scheme, the activities were more limited, focusing on a six- to 12-week enabling support programme.

City Saturday Club. This club aimed to provide activities for children with special needs and respite for their families and carers. The project was hosted by the city's well-established multi-agency team, who provided a range of other services and built on existing weekday provision.

Mid-County Saturday Club. This club also aimed to provide activities for children with special needs and respite for their families and carers. It had a large catchment area from across the mid-county area and was hosted by a well-established charitable trust that provided a similar scheme at a school for children with special needs. The project held monthly sessions for different age groups and had a structured programme of activities, ensuring a variety of experience for participants. It also provided day trips.

The second partnership area focusing on disabled children was a metropolitan authority of three towns. This partnership targeted a range of groups across the three towns, based on evidenced need within them. There were a number of general themes across the Children's Fund programme, for example 'Taking Part', and services for disabled children and children with special needs were proposed within a number of these interrelating themes. Thus, a programme of services for 'children with special needs and disabled children' was developed as the need for services within each of the towns emerged. Services were commissioned locally and separately, and were then identified as linked through their common target group. The anticipated long-term outcomes focused on children rather than families and included increased participation in services, increased confidence through participation (but also through improved familial understanding and relationships) and enabling children to gain nationally accredited qualifications that would improve their employment opportunities. Another long-term aspiration was that children who had been users of services would subsequently become involved in running services.

This second partnership also identified objectives relating to changes in mainstream service provision. The partnership aimed to improve both accessibility and sustainability of services through the creation of a comprehensive and integrated range of services, and enabling both parents and children to have a strong voice. Its rationale was that the resultant inclusive services would support disabled children. To achieve this, the projects that were commissioned were intended to fill gaps in mainstream provision and included:

Integrated Sports Project. This was hosted by a voluntary sector organisation working with disabled people. It provided after-school clubs in (four, then three) special schools across the authority and one at the organisation's own centre. A range of sports was provided, but football dominated due to the children's preferences. The aim was for children to participate and enjoy themselves. Some basic qualifications were available for participants.

Family Activity Project. This was developed by parents who applied for Children's Fund support to consolidate and expand their activities. The project provided activities for families as a unit so that they spent positive time together and with other families with a disabled child. The project provided a range of activities for families each Saturday afternoon, focused on healthy eating and lifestyles, organised trips during school holidays and provided short breaks for families.

Impacts for children and their families

In both partnerships, children, their parents or carers and workers reported benefits from services designed exclusively for disabled children *and* those that were designed to enable them to take part in mixed settings, where children felt safe and secure and were away from home. Being with others 'like them' enabled children to recognise that others shared similar experiences, as well as widening their circle of friends. There were also reports of children increasing skills and confidence as a result of specialist input. Learning and demonstrating new skills (including to their parents) was important for children whose lack of ability was often the focus of attention. In addition, parents and workers identified the positive impact of more integrationist aspects of the strategies on non-disabled children, suggesting that barriers to inclusion were being reduced. Workers seeking to enable children to take part in mainstream activities such as Brownies also reported adaptations to practices to support such inclusion, although there were also instances where children had negative experiences in attempting to access mainstream services, for example being unable to access local swimming facilities due to a lack of suitably qualified lifeguards.

Parents and carers identified positive impacts of both respite and involvement in services. Respite enabled them to spend more time with other family members as well as 'just to recharge your batteries' (Barnes et al, 2006a, p 27). Involvement was an opportunity to learn from other families, to experience the support of others with similar experiences and for the whole family to increase their understanding and improve family relationships as a result. For example, one mother of a deaf daughter described the impact on her non-disabled son: 'My son's definitely gained from mixing with other brothers and sisters who are in a similar situation to him. So that's good because ... he was very resentful of his sister for a long time' (Barnes et al, 2006a, p 27).

The evidence relating to the significance of children and young people as decision makers was more limited. They were asked and consulted about what activities they would like to do, but there was no evidence of involvement in strategic or management structures. There was limited evidence of significant participation of children in services – other than simply asking them what they would like to do. There was also little evidence to suggest that children valued activities *they* had chosen more than those suggested by staff. For parents, benefits were more likely to be the result of respite or from being service recipients than through being co-producers of services. One exception was a parent-led service in the metropolitan authority, which was a 'club' for families that provided play and organised outings. Here the level of children's involvement was higher and there was evidence that children enjoyed the process of participation in its own right and the recognition it offered them (Barnes et al, 2006a).

Impacts for services

The evaluation failed to identify any major impacts on mainstream service delivery. In the county authority the Children's Fund services were seen to have *filled a gap* in statutory provision for disabled children, but there were concerns about their sustainability beyond the funding associated with the Children's Fund. For example, as well as insecurity for particular services, there was very limited evidence of specific training for play workers in mainstream agencies. The changes achieved were insufficient to drive the long-term aim of greater inclusion within mainstream services, despite this being recognised as necessary to the achievement of objectives in both partnerships' strategies.

Evidence did suggest that some progress was achieved towards outcome objectives relating to more integrated working between agencies in relation to individual children. Children's Fund funding enabled some providers to increase the number of children and families using their services, but demand for places outstripped supply. Another aspect of accessibility related to the criteria for access. There was a view that the Children's Fund had helped lower the thresholds of need at which mainstream agencies would consider providing services, although this had caused tensions over the issue of self-referral.

The metropolitan authority's strategy had aimed to create a comprehensive range of services, involving more effective partnerships. Yet, the four Children's Fund services focusing on disabled children had little to do with each other. It was unclear whether the commissioning group had conceived what an integrated programme might look like and whether the four projects would have a role within this. The parent-led group was seen within the local authority as having paved the way in terms of consulting with parents and had contributed to the development of a borough-wide network set up by the social services department and open to any family with a child with special needs. Supporting the development of a genuinely community-led project took time and resources that were seen as beyond mainstream resources or capacity. The objective of increasing service access remained largely unrealised, in spite of efforts within individual services to improve particular aspects of accessibility. A major factor was the location of services and the availability of transport. Children studied in the evaluation came from a limited geographical area, despite the partnership covering three towns. Children using the services also had a limited range of impairments and it is doubtful that these services were reaching the most marginalised disabled children. Staff working in these four services saw their future in the Children's Trust arrangements and there was limited evidence of action to secure funding from elsewhere.

Black and minority ethnic children

In this chapter we continue to use the term 'black and minority ethnic' children as a term of convenience for a broad range of groups. The term was used within our two case study areas to refer to different groups at different times and within different services, but we are more specific in reporting the findings where possible and appropriate. We looked at provision in two cities. The larger of the two initially focused solely on 'black boys' (from African and African Caribbean backgrounds) but this was developed into a focus on boys and girls with an African or African Caribbean heritage. In the other city the focus was broader, defined as a broad 'black and minority ethnic' group, to include a range of different ethnic groups and heritage.

Although they worked in different ways to develop their strategies and in different local contexts, both partnerships defined similar outcome objectives and suggested similar rationales for the preventative activities they put in place. In both instances this was related to the underachievement of children from minority ethnic communities within formal education (something shared by both cities as well as being a pattern established across the UK (Morris et al, 2006). The common outcomes objectives shared by both partnerships included:

• securing enhanced formal educational attainment by providing additional learning opportunities based outside the traditional school setting and located within children's communities;
• enabling new experiences that engage black and minority ethnic children positively in learning and education and help them cope better with educational settings;
• providing support for children's networks in helping children navigate the formal education system and so assist in achieving better educational outcomes;
• building on and supporting community-based provision to ensure that the services accurately reflect the needs, heritage and experiences of black and minority ethnic children and offer disadvantaged families support and practical help;
• balancing negative or absent mainstream black and minority ethnic images with positive cultural images and experiences that enable children to grow in confidence and assist them in coping with racism and oppression; and
• trying to influence and change existing practices in order to achieve better services for black and minority ethnic children.

The themed approach taken in both cities and the structures put in place to support their work built on evidence of the failure of existing mainstream provision to respond adequately to the needs of black and minority ethnic children. Both partnerships made arrangements to roll out service development under the auspices of a specific black and minority ethnic task or reference group, with community groups identified as those best placed to identify need and develop appropriate provision.

In the larger city there were three services that were the focus for this work with black and minority ethnic children:

Mobile Educational Resource Project. This was hosted by the city's central library service. It aimed to provide enhanced learning for African Caribbean children by direct provision and through engagement with mainstream provision. The project experienced delays and difficulties in becoming established. A converted bus was equipped with books, instruments, arts and crafts and displays with all materials culturally relevant to African Caribbean heritage and culture and aiming to promote positive cultural images. The bus targeted supplementary schools and out-of-school play and educational provision in areas with a high representation of African Caribbean children.

Educational Arts Project. This was based within an existing community organisation for black young people that used performing arts techniques, residential trips and outings to build self-esteem through a focus on health, education and empowerment. Children's Fund funding was part of a diverse set of funding streams and support that this organisation relied on. The main activities during the evaluation period were dance and theatre performance and music and studio skills.

Community Horticultural Project. This gardening project was part of a range of horticultural activities provided by a black and minority ethnic community-based voluntary sector organisation. The project aimed to promote healthy eating and lifestyle and positive activities. It introduced children and young people to organic gardening, to the growing and harvesting of crops, to environmental concerns and to recycling. The Children's Fund was one of a range of funders supporting the organisation. Allotments were used to hold sessions for young people and to involve ex-offenders and others from the community in developing positive role models. Schools also accessed the project and children from a range of ethnic backgrounds were involved.

There were a wider range of services in the smaller city, which had defined its target group rather more broadly:

Domestic Violence Victims Project. This project targeted black and minority ethnic women and children and was delivered by a service for women who are victims of domestic violence and abuse. The project provided after-school clubs in the host project's safe-houses and a children's support worker for those being resettled. Play schemes were also provided in school holidays. The support worker agreed a support plan with children and their mother that aimed to assist them in making new friends, to help them settle in their new community and find clubs and activities and to address school-based issues.

Asian Family Education Liaison. An education liaison worker was based within a well-established community organisation providing services to the South Asian community. The worker aimed to address issues in the school and home that impacted on educational underachievement. The worker provided support for individual children and young people through drop-in sessions at local primary and secondary schools. They also provided a number of groups, for example an Asian Girls Group, and Saturday and holiday play schemes.

Asian Disabled Children's Service. Children's Fund funding supported a holiday play scheme to be developed by a well-established voluntary sector organisation providing a range of services for South Asian disabled children and their families. The play scheme provided safe and stimulating activities that were culturally sensitive and delivered in children's home languages. Outdoor activities and trips were also provided that included families. The project aimed to raise self-esteem and confidence.

Supplementary Schools. There were two supplementary schools supported by the Children's Fund. The first took place each Saturday and was for black and minority ethnic children in one area of the city. It had previously been closed due to lack of funding. Volunteers ran the school, with one qualified teacher providing the lead. The school taught maths, English and science, with lessons linked to the national curriculum. The focus was primary-level education (due to the experience of staff) and the school aimed to raise children's confidence and educational achievement. The second school took place in a different area of the city, also on Saturdays. This school worked with children of both primary and secondary school age and had a broader curriculum that was coupled with pastoral care, aiming to raise self-esteem and confidence and from this educational attainment. The school provided tuition in maths, English, science, cultural studies and music.

Asian Children's After-School Club. This was provided by a well-established community organisation working with Pakistani and South Asian families. The club was provided each night of the week and each day during school holidays, targeting primary school-age children. The holiday scheme included day trips for families. The club provided educational play and informal learning in order to raise and support educational achievement.

Youth and Family Support: Activity Coordinator. Another well-established community organisation that provided a range of activities for children, young people and families had its 'activity coordinator' post funded by the Children's Fund. The organisation worked with children, young people and their families to plan an annual programme of activities, including a summer camping holiday. Saturday and school holiday projects provided a range of activities throughout the year. The organisation aimed to broaden users' experiences and raise families' awareness through a focus on replicable activities.

These service summaries illustrate a common characteristic – the centrality of black and minority ethnic organisations from the voluntary and community sectors in implementing the strategies devised by the partnerships in both cities.

Impacts for children and families

Children and their families reported a number of positive impacts related to the emphasis on improving educational outcomes in both partnerships. Children and young people cited examples of improved performance in school work, as well as an increased ability to concentrate. They talked about being excited by learning in non-traditional settings and by the opportunities to take part in activities such as dance, drama and horticulture that would not otherwise have been available. They felt that these activities enabled them to learn specific skills with the possibility that they could progress to higher levels of study. Children clearly demonstrated a sense of achievement that increased their confidence in different contexts. Trips outside of or to venues across the city were also reported not just as enjoyable but also as making available opportunities that were closed to many children and families due to cost, transport and access, or a lack of confidence or awareness. Group excursions brought adults, children and families together.

Some children also identified the way in which these new opportunities encouraged them away from more negative behaviour: 'I was very naughty and I was getting bored of school work. I have learnt about planting vegetables and digging out weeds. My behaviour has changed because if I am not good then [learning mentor] will not let me go' (Morris et al, 2006, p 43).

Parents identified improved behaviour at home, which benefited the whole family. Shared activities also helped children develop a sense of responsibility to others and children were reported to be calmer, more prepared to apologise and to show respect to others.

The emphasis on culturally relevant resources and on role models from within the children's own communities was also showing positive effects as children were able to see positive images of black people and to recognise that they had a rich cultural heritage. In addition to this anticipated outcome there was also evidence of a broader sense of community and citizenship that had not been anticipated, as projects brought together children and families from different backgrounds either within their own provision or through links with other services where they were more tightly targeted at particular groups. The limited range of provision in the larger city led to more limited impacts and for fewer children and families than the smaller city's more comprehensive programme.

Impacts for services

Although both partnerships had defined outcome objectives relating to impacting the mainstream agencies, in reality implementation focused primarily on equipping individual children to progress within formal education systems directly or through the related effects of raised self-esteem and confidence and improved behaviour and relationships. Few if any of the projects maintained close links with mainstream organisations or were positioned to influence the provision of mainstream services. One issue dominates the analysis of the strategies: the extent to which local voluntary and community sector organisations and networks had the infrastructure and capacity to lead on the development of a themed programme of provision in the way that the strategic partnerships intended in their rationales.

The story of the services in the larger city highlights the potential dangers and limitations of this approach. In this city the development of the community-based approach was the source of highly contested accounts. There were disagreements and problems around a range of different, often interlinked, issues and events. In exploring the history of the theme with members of the community collective that was initially developed to implement the strategy, and with members of the Children's Fund partnership, we encountered a lack of both clarity and agreement about the nature of the autonomy extended to the collective to assess the needs of the children and to devise and implement the strategy. Some from outside the group challenged its claims to offer a 'community' and 'collective' approach to this work. There were also questions about the capacity of the collective to drive forward the strategy and simultaneously meet the regulatory and management requirements of the Children's Fund. Members of the collective felt that there was a lack of support to enable it to develop and deliver a large-scale, complex attempt to address the needs of African Caribbean boys. As the partnership's focus moved beyond African Caribbean boys to a broader target of minority ethnic groups, there was disagreement over the role of the collective in developing and supporting this change. There were also criticisms of the inadequacy of processes put in place to support the work and to ensure that emerging learning fed into broader developments within the partnership, programme and beyond into mainstream provision in the city.

As a result, the initial strategy collapsed, leaving in its wake much ill-will and bitterness among the black and minority ethnic organisations that had been involved in the collective, those that had been excluded from it, as well as those that had been involved in tendering for or proposing services and provision. The demise of the original arrangements meant that the strategy became one led from the centre of the partnership itself and became one focused on ensuring scrutiny, accountability and the maintenance of the disparate group of services.

In the smaller city an existing black voluntary and community sector organisation led the development of the themed programme. A group of services and stakeholders was drawn together and local providers were asked to submit proposals for how they might take forward the aims the partnership had established for the theme. All those who submitted a proposal that met the criteria were allocated funding, with negotiation over the level so that all could be supported. The integrity of the programme was affected by the changes to the Children's Fund nationally (as with others) as at two different points services were subject to review and reduced funding, with some being cut altogether.

This commissioning group was developed into a forum for all of those developing and delivering services within the theme. The group was involved in reviewing the progress of services and making decisions about cuts and reduced funding in a process that was agreed by all involved to be fair and transparent. As the programme matured, the group was involved in a reorganisation with other local and Children's Fund networks to form a generic black and minority ethnic children and family services network for the city's Children's Trust arrangements as the need for integration and mainstreaming was addressed.

These two accounts of the histories of the partnerships' approaches indicate that, despite the commonality in objectives and rationale of the two strategies, there were considerable differences in delivery and in the outcomes achieved.

Gypsy/Traveller children

Once again, we use the term 'Gypsy/Traveller' as a shorthand term to include a range of different groups who follow a travelling lifestyle. Our focus here was on a consortium of Children's Fund partnerships in one region. The underlying rationale of the consortium approach was that this would enable consistency of service development while reflecting the mobility of the children and families targeted. The consortium's work focused on Irish Travellers and English Gypsies as these were the two largest groups across the region, but it did aim to be inclusive of other groups (for example fairground people).

The consortium commissioned a service from a large voluntary agency with experience of working with Gypsy/Traveller children and their families. 'Development officers' were recruited to work with children, linking with teachers from the region's Traveller Education Service who agreed to provide links to sites and families housed within settled communities. Linked to its strategy there were four areas of activity:

Work with local play providers to ensure that their provision was inclusive of Gypsy/Traveller children

This activity targeted mainstream and other service providers to advocate for the needs of Gypsy/Traveller children and young people for play and leisure opportunities, and provide cultural awareness training. The aim was to establish a greater consistency of inclusive provision across the region through this and partnership work with providers. The Traveller Education Service provided cultural awareness training for a (small) number of providers, for example a youth centre and play service. The development officers also worked to create links between themselves and providers of leisure and play activities. Development officers visited providers and discussed with them the needs of local Gypsy/Traveller children and young people and negotiated access or secured explicit agreement that they would not be excluded. In practice, this part of the project, beyond the negotiation of immediate access, took a secondary role to the core area of activity identified below.

Work with parents and families to raise awareness of local play provision and to develop confidence in accessing services

The project aimed to raise awareness among Gypsy/Traveller parents and families of available services and of their rights to access them. There was an assumption that families were wary of mainstream services developed for the settled community and that by supporting access, positive experiences would build confidence and sustain involvement. Development officers provided information to parents about general local provision, for example during summer holidays, and in some instances negotiated access for Gypsy/Traveller children and families with providers. By supporting children and young people in accessing services the development officers demonstrated that local provision could be inclusive.

Direct work with children and young people

The core element of the strategy was direct work with children and young people. The rationale for this was that supported access would build children's confidence and self-esteem and that positive experiences would encourage them to seek out other opportunities without support. Thus, the project aimed to enable children and young people to access leisure and play provision in order to have more contact with non-Traveller children and to have positive experiences. Development officers conducted assessments of children's interests with children and their families and identified locally available provision in response to this. They also provided small amounts of funding to support access, for example purchasing equipment for sports activities. The main part of the development officers' work was supporting Gypsy/Traveller children and young people in accessing local provision. They found that there was extremely limited participation in local services and they worked to provide supported access beyond raising awareness of availability. One example of this was providing transport for a group of children from a site to attend a local play service twice a week. Another example was taking housed Gypsy/Traveller children to swimming sessions. Development officers would accompany groups of children to local youth and play provision. By providing this intensive supported access, the project aimed to raise confidence within families and thus encourage and enable families to access these services without support.

Work to counter negative portrayals and stereotypes of Gypsy/ Traveller culture within the settled community

This final area of work was always recognised as a secondary activity, and that the aimed-for outcomes could only be achieved as a consequence of the core roles of raising awareness among service providers and supporting positive and inclusive activities, rather than as a result of discrete targeted activity. Development officers challenged local providers who excluded Gypsies/Travellers (although this was rarely explicit exclusion) but also supported parents in accessing and attending local planning and other forums. For example, a local health service review was attended by a group of parents, who were supported in raising their concerns about a lack of health provision for their site.

The strategy amended

Following a review of the work of the consortium (to which the evaluation contributed) the strategy was amended. Some partnerships had already decided to withdraw from the consortium and the revised approach was in part a pragmatic response to this. One conclusion was that it was as important to work with existing regional structures to 'bend the mainstream' as it was to deliver a new service. The revised theory of change also gave a higher profile to the direct involvement of Gypsy/Traveller children and families in determining the nature of services most likely to support their inclusion, and to children's rights work. Underpinning this was a realisation that although the supported access, or 'handholding', approach was enabling some children to have positive experiences of services, most work had been focused on taking children to existing services, rather than trying to change the nature of those services. The sustainability of the initial strategy was considered to be vulnerable without this outside focus. Thus, the revised theory of change represented a change in the balance of activity, although the overall approach remained one of increasing use of mainstream services as a route to social inclusion.

Impacts for children and families

There was evidence that the aim of building confidence and self-esteem among children was achieved in the short to medium term. Parents and development officers felt that children had grown in confidence and children talked proudly of new skills, such as swimming, that they had acquired. There was not much to do on sites and children benefited from being taken off the site. One girl said 'when [development officer] comes it is like the sun shining' (Mason et al, 2006, p 41). But a number of factors limited the effectiveness of the strategy, primarily relating to the dominance of 'handholding' activities to the near exclusion of other elements and in particular a failure to build capacity in the mainstream. And the handholding itself was not without difficulties. It was difficult to plan activities with any confidence that children would be on site or that parents would be there to give consent to their children leaving the site so that some children would miss out. Consequently, in some cases, groups were not able to attend full sessions, due to these organisational difficulties and to transport limitations. In several areas, taxis refused to take children because they were Gypsies/Travellers; and some taxis refused to take children following bad behaviour. Children generally did not understand that supporting their access to activities, or those organised especially for them, was funded for a short time only and the failure to link effectively with mainstream provision meant that the service was seen as setting up and then withdrawing, repeating a history of short-term provision for, and work with, these communities.

Parents were rarely actively resistant to their children taking part in activities. Indeed, parents made positive comments about the activities providing exercise, enjoyment and opportunities to learn. The concerns parents reported to development officers and researchers about children entering mixed settings were about their vulnerability and protecting them from situations they perceived as being potentially dangerous, rather than about not valuing opportunities or fearing culture loss. Some of these fears were being overcome. For example, one mother said: 'sometimes you say, right I'll go to the swimming pool, but I didn't want to go because the kids might call them names and I don't want to be putting the kids through that. Now I realise they don't really, nobody says anything to them' (Mason et al, 2006, p 43).

Development officers built trusting relationships with parents who became more aware of what services were available. Workers' preparedness to take on advocacy and other supportive roles on behalf of parents was considered to help to build such relationships. While both parents and children reported benefits from the activities they were able to engage in through the Children's Fund service, there was little evidence that this was leading to children seeking out other activities and thus that the impacts of the strategy were likely to be sustainable. Interviews indicated a number of barriers to further involvement:

- income levels and the cost of leisure activities;
- mothers' wish for respite rather than involvement;
- lack of spare time available for mothers to support their children's involvement;
- lack of suitable and accessible transport;
- lack of basic skills (such as literacy); and
- family priorities, for example over the use of the family car or travelling commitments.

Impacts for services

The original strategy identified the need for change in mainstream services and this was given greater emphasis following the consortium's mid-term review. The way in which work with other agencies developed varied across the partnerships involved in the consortium. This was because of differences in the Gypsy/Traveller communities, in the services available in local authority areas, the geographical location of sites and the existence of networks of service providers working with Gypsies/Travellers. Not all Children's Fund partnerships from across the region were involved and thus a regional approach was never developed. This limited further the organisational change and impact the strategy intended, as there was no sustained capacity across the region working for change. The aspiration of creating a regional group that would offer a strategic overview of services for Gypsy/Traveller children and families was not realised.

Refugee and asylum-seeking children and families

The two partnerships we studied in this regard were a city metropolitan authority and a London borough. In the metropolitan authority the focus was developed into a broad definition of 'newly arrived' families to include those arriving from the European Union as well as migrants from elsewhere in the world. The London borough focused on refugees and asylum seekers as defined in legal terms but also the children of immigrants (who we define as second-generation communities). These communities were targeted as they were seen to suffer from exclusion from mainstream services, provision and the broader community more generally.

The city authority defined the objectives of its strategy for newly arrived children and families as:

- supporting integration into school and improving educational attainment. This was a response to the schools' identified needs for support in meeting the needs of newly arrived children as well as families' needs for support in accessing and flourishing within school;
- improving the mental health and well-being of refugee and asylum-seeking children and families: to help children deal with issues arising from trauma, bereavement and loss they may have suffered but also to help families settle into their new lives;
- supporting newly arrived families: by brokering access to services, advocating, and providing responsive family support; and
- raising capacity within mainstream and other service providers: by promoting and facilitating multi-agency working and raising the profile of newly arrived families through advocacy and targeted awareness-raising.

The following services were commissioned to achieve these outcomes:

Responsive Family Support: This service was hosted by a black-led voluntary sector agency. It aimed to provide intensive and tailored support for newly arrived families in order to enable them to access mainstream and voluntary and community sector services, including schools and health services. The service offered negotiated packages of support, brokerage and advocacy. The project also targeted service providers for awareness raising and training and worked with a large number of mainstream, voluntary and private (landlords) organisations and agencies.

Support for Children's Emotional and Trauma Needs. This project was based within the local education authority. It provided art therapy, horticultural therapy, play therapy and individual counselling for children referred through schools. By providing therapeutic support, the project aimed to enable children to overcome distress and trauma associated with their experiences. By taking referrals from schools, who were carefully introduced to the project and assessment criteria, the project aimed to improve children's integration and their educational achievement.

School Integration Support: This project was also located within the local education authority. The project was based around a cluster of schools and provided support for newly arrived children, working in partnership with the Responsive Family Support and the Emotional and Trauma Needs services. As with those services, the project aimed to improve integration, raise self-esteem and improve educational attainment. The service worked with schools that had limited experience of supporting newly arrived children, by raising awareness and providing specialist support. The service withdrew from schools when it was agreed with them that they had gained enough experience and expertise to function without ongoing support.

Extended School Support Team. This was also hosted by the local education authority but located within an Extended School. The project aimed to provide a multi-agency approach to support families' transition and induction to living in the city, by linking families to appropriate provision and aiming, over time, to empower families to live independently. The project built on the experiences of the Responsive Family Support and School Integration Support projects to offer multi-agency support from one centre. Links with the Emotional and Trauma Needs project ensured that those children suffering from trauma and distress received appropriate therapeutic support.

The London borough defined the objectives of its strategy for newly arrived children and families as to:

- promote and improve emotional well-being of refugee and asylum-seeking children and young people;
- raise the educational attainment of refugee and asylum-seeking children and young people;
- improve community cohesion and integration;
- change practice.

Key to the development of the strategy was the employment of a development officer, to commission services that would deliver these outcomes. The other central strand was funding for a minority ethnic community-led group working to address educational underachievement and the involvement in crime of young men, in particular, from the community. Parents had come together and worked with young people to identify their concerns and the support and provision they would like. This included homework support but also drop-in advice sessions for families, for example where parents felt unable to support their child in school and where they could receive advice on available and appropriate provision.

The development officer commissioned a number of projects to deliver the outcomes:

Art Therapy Project. This was commissioned following a piloting period in response to concerns about the emotional well-being of refugee and asylum-seeking children. Schools were selected following the piloting in community settings, as they were the sites where children were exhibiting problems and as places where confidential and private space could be provided. Two art therapists provided support for referred children and young people, aiming to address problems associated with trauma and distress.

Music Therapy Project. This project was commissioned with the same rationale as Art Therapy, but extended existing Primary Care Trust provision to a new target group. The service was group and non-issue-based, and worked with children referred by their schools.

Library After-School Club. This club was set within the library of one of the borough's town halls in recognition of its central location, accessibility and potential for wider benefits for families introduced to the library itself. The club ran twice each week, aiming to support and promote children's access to books and resources. Enjoyable and creative activities included information technology-based work.

Literacy Project. This was based within a community organisation working with a particular ethnic group that had a history of working with first- and second-generation migrants. The local education authority identified children from this minority ethnic community as underachieving at school and the Saturday Literacy Project was a response to this. The organisation provided a range of other activities (see 'Football' below), mixing culturally appropriate learning with activities to strengthen cultural identity.

Football Project. This was based within the same centre as the Literacy Project and was commissioned in response to both the lack of sports activities available for young people and particularly young men in this part of the borough, and to the lack of engagement of this particular minority ethnic community. The Saturday Football Project was open to all, encouraging a mix of children and young people from across the borough.

Arts Project. This one-off project with second-generation refugees took place within a local school where their underachievement had been identified by the 'ethnic minority achievement co-ordinator'. The project aimed to raise self-esteem and confidence through a participative arts project that explored the different cultural backgrounds and heritage of pupils at the school. The films produced were used as a centrepiece to Refugee Week and acted as a catalyst for activity within the school to support first- and second-generation refugee children.

Impacts for children and families

Children and parents reported positive impacts resulting from support for children's integration into school and improvements in their educational attainment. In addition to support with school enrolment that some projects offered newly arrived families, parents appreciated the advocacy services provided, which aimed to ensure that schools fulfil their statutory duty of providing school places for newly arrived children and providing support for children with English as an additional language.

In the city authority, where the primary emphasis of the partnership was on the induction of newly arrived children into school and subsequent support in this context, children talked of ways in which projects had helped them to understand school routines, develop their English language skills, build their self-esteem and confidence, improve their social and emotional literacy skills and make new friends. In the London borough, children and parents provided evidence of the positive impact of after-school clubs, which offered a space to do homework, and provided help with literacy, numeracy, information technology and other subjects. There was evidence that encouraging children from different backgrounds to mix had been effective.

Some children attending therapeutic services portrayed these as safe spaces to discuss current or past experiences and feelings and to gradually explore alternative ways of dealing with them. Most shared memories of the fun times they had, indicating that the therapy-based projects offered them respite from their emotional problems without any pressure to resolve them. Children and parents also reported improved emotional well-being as a result of the practical and emotional support they received in accessing and making effective use of mainstream services and developing their social networks.

There was a wealth of evidence that indicated the importance of support that aimed to overcome or reduce some of the barriers to social inclusion, for instance with language and literacy, that newly arrived families faced. While refugee families treasured the individually tailored support that projects in the city authority provided, those in the London borough indicated the added value of pursuing this objective within a community context that enabled the development of social networks. In addition to fostering a sense of belonging and community, these networks were portrayed as promoting the cultural resources and coping strategies that refugees and asylum seekers could draw on to mitigate the effects and dynamics of social exclusion.

Impacts for services

Evidence suggested that the strategy in the city authority was particularly successful in raising schools' awareness of the multiple factors potentially impacting on young refugees' abilities to integrate into new schools; and in actively exploring with them holistic approaches to addressing these factors. The services commissioned to deliver the strategy shared responsibility for information sharing, training and awareness raising, ensuring that the work gained a high profile. This structured approach was largely absent from the London borough's programme. The particular location of the development officer post within the education department seemed to push refugees and asylum seekers higher up the education service agenda, but the extent to which this profile would be sustained beyond the existence of the post was unclear. For instance, there was no clear commitment to the support of the out-of-school projects nor to the therapeutic support projects. The programme of services was more isolated from mainstream practice and emerging developments under the Every Child Matters framework than those in the city authority where a sustained network of provision worked to maintain their profile and influence.

Conclusion: changing children or challenging barriers?

Children and families described and demonstrated a range of positive outcomes and impacts as a result of the targeted strategies presented here. Across each of the target groups we worked with, the specialist, targeted provision that was developed and supported was highly valued by users. Children's Fund programmes filled gaps in mainstream and existing provision, provided new opportunities and raised self-esteem. Family support helped address issues for parents, siblings and the family as a unit as well as the child or young person that was most often the 'target' of provision. Reflecting the sub-objectives of the Children's Fund, educational attainment and achievement were often the focus of strategies, and both formal and informal learning had positive impacts that were valued by children, young people and families. Advocacy and signposting to other services also led to benefits for service users. In some cases, participation and consultation were an important element of successful provision and approaches to service and programme development. But meaningful participation takes time to develop and, for some children and families, more pressing and immediate needs negated the extent to which such participation was considered worthwhile or appropriate.

These strategies were intended to influence the way in which mainstream services operated as well as to produce direct benefits for those using Children's Fund services. Here the impacts were less clear. There were two aspects to this. First, as we have noted, many of the services were commissioned from local community and voluntary agencies or groups. In these instances it was possible to build on local knowledge and expertise within the voluntary and community sectors, but such groups often lacked the scope or ability to develop provision as intended. The required capacity-building work is time consuming and costly and not always possible where there are pressures to develop and deliver services. Second, Children's Fund projects, services and activities were successfully filling gaps in provision but were having limited impact on the way in which mainstream services were operating. This was also an impact on their sustainability. Services were vulnerable as a result of their time-limited funding. Children's Fund provision was not mainstream provision and limited mainstream budgets were not able to accommodate this new, preventative practice. Networks between services, learning and mainstream change all took resources and it was not possible to support such change where these were limited. Direct service provision took priority over this more developmental approach, often as a result of the pressing need for services for marginalised groups who lacked appropriate targeted provision or who experienced mainstream services as inaccessible and exclusionary. We explore these issues more fully in Chapter Seven; but it is important to recognise in concluding here that the positive impacts that Children's Funds' targeted provision was able to achieve were limited to the level of individual children, young people and sometimes their families rather than sustainable change in preventative provision.

These findings were echoed across the full analysis of evidence gathered by the evaluation (Edwards et al 2006). The final reports prepared by the evaluation drew together findings from the full range of strands within the evaluation design. This analysis revealed that children and families, often with immediate and pressing needs, welcomed targeted provision. But without sustainable change to mainstream provision, long-term impacts were unlikely to be either achieved or maintained. Developmental work with services was often an aspiration rather than a focus for activity, and change programmes devised by partnerships had their integrity affected by changes to funding and other commitments from the outset of the national programme. Holistic, responsive family provision emerged across our findings as the approach most valued by children and families. This long-term sustained support from caseworkers, or work underpinned by a casework approach, was highly valued. Such approaches included supporting access to and advocacy within mainstream and existing provision. But these service-level activities were often at the expense of activity directed towards achieving change in service structures beyond those funded through the Children's Fund.

Practical support and frontline provision was required by marginalised groups who traditionally had found their needs un(der)-recognised and un(der)-addressed. This was particularly true of provision that was culturally appropriate and respectful of individual, family and community strengths. Targeted provision was highly valued but children and families shared an aspiration with those who had designed strategies – indeed in some instances this was related to their involvement in their design – that inclusive mainstream provision was required if social exclusion was to be meaningfully addressed. Without achieving systemic change, individual- and family-level impacts remained limited to attempts to equip marginalised groups with the capacity to resist exclusionary processes rather than targeting those processes themselves.

In the next chapter we explore what these strategies and services suggest about approaches to prevention, and the assumptions that underpinned these approaches.

SEVEN

New understandings for prevention

Introduction

In this book we have explored the way in which policies for children and families in the UK have evolved, considered key concepts that have undermined these developments – in particular social exclusion and prevention – and examined in more detail the implementation of one such policy – the Children's Fund. This chapter begins by drawing together the evidence described in the preceding chapter with the framework of the dimensions of social exclusion set out in Chapter Two, and reflects on what this suggests for an overall analysis of the impact of the Children's Fund in this context. As Chapter Four described, prevention and early intervention are now set firmly within a context of a political analysis of social exclusion and its consequences. The Children's Fund was one example of a raft of national preventative initiatives and its overall objectives were clearly located within the aspiration to reduce the impact of social exclusion: 'The Children's Fund is a central part of the Government's agenda for children and families and aims to make a real difference to the lives of children and young people at risk of social exclusion' (CYPU, 2001b, p 2).

Despite the central guidance offered by the-then governing unit (the Children and Young People's Unit; CYPU), the data gathered by the National Evaluation of the Children's Fund (NECF) suggested that the Children's Fund can only be fully understood by looking closely at the complexity and diversity of local implementation. Local partnerships adopted different approaches to the analysis of needs, to defining ways of targeting their activities, to understanding the experiences of children and families and to the more precise definition of intended outcomes. The analysis of data generated by NECF has therefore provided opportunities for new analyses of the way in which both policy makers and practitioners understand prevention when set within the context of social exclusion.

The data also allow for an assessment of the effect of the different approaches that were evident in practice within the partnership case studies considered in Chapters Five and Six. In this chapter we begin by setting the analysis of the Children's Fund data against the dimensions of social exclusion discussed in Chapter Two to offer a commentary on the effectiveness of the initiative within a social exclusion framework. We then present an overall analysis of the different types of preventative approaches evident in the activities of those implementing the Children's Fund and consider the implications of these different approaches for preventative policies and practices more generally.

Dimensions of social exclusion: evidence of impact

While *The Children's Fund Guidance* (CYPU, 2001b) did not utilise the dimensions of social exclusion that we have adopted, it *was* concerned with how the poor outcomes for children and families at risk of social exclusion could be addressed. We have discussed in earlier chapters the translation of the wide-ranging objectives of the Fund into child-level indicators that shifted the focus of the initiative from broad social issues to individual attainments and changes. It is therefore of value to consider how a national initiative concerned with social exclusion was able to address the range of exclusionary processes facing children and their families.

Material

Material dimensions of exclusion relate to income poverty, access to goods and activities, and the condition of physical environments. Evidence from NECF confirmed that the strategies developed and activities put in place in the case study authorities reported here did not focus on raising the incomes of families in poverty in any direct way. Nonetheless, there were some initiatives that mitigated some of the impacts of poverty. For example, after- and out-of-school provision provided in the smaller city where services for black and minority ethnic families were our focus did aim to provide childcare for working parents. Also, advice and advocacy services for refugee and asylum-seeking families aimed to raise awareness of benefit and support entitlement. These families were severely lacking material resources and the services offered within these Children's Fund strategies worked to ensure that families could access items such as linen and household goods, as well as school uniforms and other items. There was some provision of goods for Gypsy/Traveller children and young people, for example in order to enable them to take part in certain leisure activities.

And there was provision of goods in the form of culturally relevant resources for some of the minority ethnic communities.

Notwithstanding these examples, the primary focus of the Children's Fund strategies that we have explored was the provision of *activities* that had been denied to the target groups or that they had difficulty in accessing and experienced as exclusionary. We have seen how separate activity provision was developed, for example for disabled and Gypsy/Traveller children and families as well as the development of supported access that aimed to link these groups to existing provision. Activity also aimed to build capacity within existing provision, through raising awareness or delivering training in order to improve access to children living in deprived circumstances. But as we have seen, there was a mixed picture within individual strategies as well as across the range of strategies considered. Therefore, when set against the material dimension of social exclusion, we can see that the Children's Fund had a very partial emphasis, focusing on only one aspect of this dimension. Little activity was directed towards changing the financial well-being of the families, or the physical environments within which they lived. Indeed, the Guidance placed limits on the use of funding so that repairing damp properties or building social housing would have not been feasible.

Spatial

Spatial dimensions relate to restrictions on where people can live and their mobility within and between places. The regional strategy for Gypsy/Traveller children and families aimed to provide a structure for service provision that was responsive to the movements of families across the region; as we saw in our analysis, this was never achieved. Yet, the strategy did attempt to ameliorate some of the negative effects Gypsy/Traveller families experienced as a result of living (often) on sites that lacked basic amenities and were physically isolated from the settled community and mainstream (and other) service structures. In revising its strategy, and recognising the limits to the sustainability of the activity focus of its initial approach, the regional consortium aimed to link Gypsy/Traveller families more effectively into local planning and other structures so that issues relating to their geographical isolation could be addressed.

One of the partnership strategies for refugee and asylum-seeking families also had an explicit aim to address issues relating to the locales and neighbourhoods where families were placed. The family support service advocated for families where accommodation was unsuitable and also supported them in challenging decisions and reporting racism. This effort to improve the experience of living in deprived areas and in places where exclusionary attitudes and poor resources contributed to the overall experience of deprivation and social exclusion was a feature of a number of aspects of the strategies we explored. By providing activities, attempting to bring services into areas where they had not traditionally worked, providing access to services where they were geographically dispersed and developing new multi-agency configurations, strategies aimed to change the experience of living in excluded communities – even if this could not include addressing barriers to mobility and movement.

The strategies for disabled children demonstrated very little attention to the physical barriers that contribute to and maintain exclusion. Provision did not address these barriers beyond time-limited support to enable access. Services were also clustered around special schools, with no attention given to the difficulties for children in accessing provision when it was often sited considerable distances from their home. By failing to address the problems faced by those without cars and reliant on public transport – which in rural areas was often irregular as well as inaccessible for those with restricted mobility – services were unlikely to reach the most marginalised disabled children.

Access to goods and services

This dimension relates to access to goods, in part relating to features of the first dimension, but importantly also to private, statutory and non-statutory services. Central to much of the work of the Children's Fund was the direct provision of services for marginalised groups, supported access to existing services (across sectors) and work to raise capacity within services to meet specific needs of excluded children and families. As with the above dimensions, there was a mixed picture of evidence of impact within individual strategies as well as across the work of the Children's Fund as a whole. We have seen how impacts were achieved in the delivery of services and also in supporting access. But we have also seen how these bespoke and piecemeal services were vulnerable where they were fixed term and wholly or mostly dependent on Children's Fund partnerships for financial support. Difficulties in demonstrating impact against changing priorities were a key concern. Changes to available funding resulted in services often being short term in nature and this also limited their impact, with questions over the sustainability of this specialist provision (largely provided from within the voluntary and community sector) once Children's Fund support came to an end. There were some instances of capacity building taking place within mainstream agencies, for example in the city where the strategy for refugee and asylum-seeking families was our focus, and in both partnerships targeting disabled children. Yet this capacity building was often only a limited part of the focused services' activity rather than a separate and discreet strategy in its own right. Thus, such activity was vulnerable to financial and policy changes or was difficult to achieve within limited resources and where demand for frontline provision was high.

Health and well-being

This relates to the negative impacts on physical and emotional health and general well-being that can result from exclusionary processes, structures and experiences. Evidence from NECF indicates that one feature of the strategies for refugee and asylum-seeking children and families was the provision of services with a direct impact on emotional health and well-being. A range of therapeutic services for children formed a central feature of each strategy. These services also worked to link families with National Health Service (NHS) provision, for example in ensuring access to general practitioner services, and the Gypsy/Traveller activities also included some advocacy with local health services where families articulated negative and exclusionary experiences.

A concern with well-being more generally was a feature of all of the strategies we focused on. They contained explicit aims to provide enjoyment, raise self-esteem, improve well-being and raise individuals' sense of self and pride in the community and cultural heritage, and (in two strategies) to counter negative associations with disability. The evidence of impact within this broad conception of well-being often relied on testimony from children and young people and their families and about the benefits they felt from participation in services that previously had not existed or that they had been unable to access, as well as their reported physical benefits from involvement in play and leisure opportunities. Where tensions within families were addressed, either directly through family support or as a result of issues for children and young people being addressed by targeted provision, improvements to family experience and family dynamics resulted in reported positive impacts on well-being for the family as a unit and not just individuals themselves. Across the targeted groups that we worked with, enjoyment was key to positive impacts on well-being. However, the extent to which key strategic health stakeholders became involved in the management boards of the initiative was limited and uneven. There was very little action intended to combat directly the effects of poverty and disadvantage on physical health (such as asthma), to deal directly with issues such as child obesity or to work with health service providers to improve the accessibility of child health services. As a result, the Children's Fund struggled to build significant changes into the delivery of health-based services to marginalised families and communities.

Cultural

This dimension relates to the negative associations afforded to certain minority lifestyles, cultures and circumstances and the exclusion that results from this. This aspect of social exclusion was relevant to all the groups we have considered here. The regional strategy for Gypsy/Traveller children and families included the aim of work with the settled community to address prejudice and racism. But as we have seen, this was always an aspiration, with positive outcomes intended as a result of activity that linked Gypsy/Traveller children and families with existing provision. The hope was that the settled community would have their perceptions changed through meeting Gypsies/Travellers in joint and shared activities and that service providers would receive targeted awareness training. The lack of sustained focus in this area meant that impacts on the settled community were negligible, although interviews with service providers indicated that negative perceptions had been addressed through their experiences of working with Gypsy/Traveller children and families as well as the limited amounts of awareness training provided.

More broadly, strategies targeting specific minority communities contained activity with and provision for children, young people (and families) that aimed to strengthen cultural identity, enhance self-confidence and develop personal pride in heritage while raising awareness among others. Culturally appropriate resources and provision celebrated diversity and minority heritage, and were often linked to aims to raise self-esteem and enhance children's well-being. Strategies for disabled children included activities for disabled children but also activities for mixed groups, which aimed both to strengthen identity and to counter negative perceptions and exclusionary processes. The data gathered indicate that children in particular welcomed these opportunities and responded positively to the experiences they afforded. However, there was limited evidence of changes in the negative images and stereotypes held by surrounding communities or of any broader celebration of specific community strengths occurring. Likewise, the data show limited changes to mainstream frameworks for positively understanding the culture and heritage of the marginalised communities we studied.

Self-determination and decision making

These dimensions relate to the extent to which groups, communities and individuals within them are able to take decisions about life choices or participate in and contribute to decisions that impact on their lives. Participation was a central theme of the Children's Fund from the outset and this was reflected across the work of partnerships in all the areas we studied. Partnerships had involved communities, service users and voluntary and community groups to varying degrees in the development of their strategies and services, although much of the strategic direction was determined by professional opinion and assumptions, or analyses, of need. For example, the Gypsy/Traveller regional strategy was developed without involvement of Gypsy/ Traveller communities. Yet this, and each of the other strategies considered, also contained a commitment to working with target groups within services and provision to determine features of delivery. Learning from the Gypsy/Traveller strategy indicated that greater involvement of Gypsy/Traveller communities from the outset could have resulted in a more effective strategy to address their social exclusion. The revised strategy, produced towards the end of our involvement, was developed with a number of families and was focused much more on participation and attempts to engage the communities with service configurations in a more structured way.

The other way in which partnerships sought to involve communities in developing responsive services was through the engagement of voluntary and community organisations in rolling out the strategies and services. The two partnership strategies we focused on that targeted black and minority ethnic communities aimed to 'empower' those communities through support for voluntary and community organisations, but with very different results. These approaches held considerable learning for the engagement of marginalised communities in service development, and the extent to which the desire to engage local communities could be experienced as exploitative and undermining, thereby reinforcing exclusionary processes – albeit unintentionally.

The strategies for disabled children, black and minority communities, refugee and asylum-seeking children and families and Gypsies/Travellers all aimed to enable children, young people and families to make choices and influence decisions. Strategies aimed to increase the sense of self-efficacy as well as well-being among their target groups. Evidence indicated positive impacts, although the sustainability of these and of changes in service and practitioner cultures in the longer term were less clear. Often, decision making was limited to choices of activity or forms of provision and there was limited evidence of sustained work to link marginalised groups with strategic and planning structures or to support autonomous action to resist the broader impact of discrimination or disadvantage. Work to support the involvement of voluntary sector groups and to bring them together in practice and other forums were received positively. The experiences within the Children's Fund highlight the potential for participation to contribute to prevention. Yet they also mirror the broader complexity of participation and prevention as concepts that are complex and contested, with a resultant lack of clarity about how to implement participation and prevention strategies in practice (Evans and Spicer, 2008).

This overview of the extent to which Children's Fund activity addressed these dimensions of social exclusion illustrates the limited way in which long-term and sustainable change could be achieved. In spite of the expressed objective of reducing the risk of exclusion, the emphasis on a concept of prevention defined by reference to assumed levels of need for specific services did not encourage partnerships to develop holistic strategies capable of addressing the multidimensional nature of the processes of exclusion. Although there was considerable evidence of short- and some medium-term benefits being experienced by those children and families using services, it was far from clear that these benefits would be sustained in the long term. There was also limited evidence of mainstream agencies being 'bent' and adopting practices that would pick up where the Children's Fund left off and build on those positive changes that were taking place.

Understandings of prevention

The Children's Fund was expected to be concerned with 'stopping bad things getting worse'. The Guidance issued to those engaged in taking forward the work of the Children's Fund (CYPU, 2001b) suggested that a focus at Levels Two and Three of the model of prevention adopted by the CYPU would be appropriate (see Chapter Four for a discussion of this model). Local partnerships used this tiered framework for prevention to inform their commissioning and service development – often generating internal debates within the partnership about the 'fit' between a service and the appropriate level of prevention, as illustrated in the following quote from a member of a Children's Fund Partnership Board:

> Initially there was an enormous gap between interpretations. Social Services saw prevention at the point of entry into care and the voluntary sector and young people's services saw it as Level One and Two. Play and Youth had little concept of targeted work; [for them] prevention is [about] having activities ... the voluntary sector had more concept of outcome-focused intervention but were also extremely committed to the open access, community-owned strength by involvement model of prevention. A clear split between the idea of prevention being working on risk and deficit and, identifying what the problems are and helping to tackle them and the model where prevention is building on strengths.... Now there is overall good agreement that Children's Fund prevention should mean Level Two/Three, and we are moving to working out shared outcomes for children who are Level Two. (Morris and Spicer, 2003, p 8)

The evidence from NECF indicated that the original framework for understanding and developing preventative services presented considerable limitations, when applied by local policy makers and practitioners, to the diversity and changing intensity of children and families' needs (NECF, 2004). For example, children who were the target of Children's Fund activity presented a range of needs simultaneously: refugee children often had concurrent needs that included access to a school, access to general practitioner registration and support capable of responding to the impact of their difficult experiences. These needs were set within a local context, and within operational and strategic assumptions about the processes for inclusion and intended outcomes.

Our analysis based on the empirical data generated by NECF suggested that the tiered model of levels of prevention that was adapted by the CYPU had two limitations. First, it was defined primarily by reference to preventing the need to use more intensive levels of services, rather than by the objective of preventing social exclusion. The changing policy context meant that, without reference to social exclusion and exclusionary processes, the frameworks for understanding prevention failed to reflect the wider policy shift that was concerned with the risks of social exclusion. And second, children and families who were subject to social exclusion faced diverse problems of varying intensity. They might simultaneously be located at different points on the 'prevention spectrum' in relation to, for example, their need for health services to respond to complex health needs resulting from physical impairments, and lower-level support to prevent family stress and breakdown.

In practice, these difficulties generated a variety of responses from practitioners, in part reflecting different philosophies and starting points of different agencies as indicated in the quote above. An analysis of these responses has enabled us to produce another way of conceptualising prevention, which links service strategies to social inclusion outcomes, and enables assumptions about the role and function of the state to be revealed. Thus, it offers an updated version of the original analysis provided by Hardiker et al (1991). We identified six categories from the analysis of the approaches being applied within the context of the Children's Fund (Morris and Barnes, 2008; Barnes and Morris, 2008).

Integration

This approach aims to integrate the child into existing mainstream provision – this is seen to be the most effective route to achieving better outcomes for the child. It is assumed that existing services are basically adequate and helpful and their objective is to promote and create effective citizens within a largely benign social order. Social exclusion is therefore addressed by changing the child's behaviour or building their confidence (and possibly that of their families) to enable engagement with mainstream provision. The work of the Gypsy/Traveller consortium offers an example of this. As we saw in Chapter Six, the central activity of the Gypsy/Traveller consortium service was supporting children and young people to access mainstream leisure and play provision. The rationale was explicit in targeting the assumed reluctance of Gypsy/Traveller communities to access mainstream services on the assumption that, by working with families, confidence would be developed through positive experiences gained through supported access to, for example, sports and leisure facilities. Entrenched negative attitudes among the settled community, and exclusionary processes and structures experienced by Gypsies/Travellers, were recognised to contribute to their social exclusion. Research literature supports this (Hester, 2004). Yet, by targeting families and seeking to change the children rather than services themselves, the project failed to address these broader structural and attitudinal dimensions. As a result, once supported access was withdrawn, the participation of the families in mainstream provision decreased markedly. The project relied on the central premise that children and families needed greater awareness of and confidence in mainstream provision and did not address the causes of their exclusion beyond seeking to promote positive experiences of using the service.

Adaptation

This approach is based on adapting and changing service provision to better meet the needs of groups of children who are understood not to be well serviced by existing provision. The assumption is that children will be able to achieve better outcomes if the responsiveness and flexibility of services are increased. This approach sees existing provision as needing extending and diversifying, but assumes that social exclusion can be addressed by enhancing mainstream provision so that it can be accessed by marginalised children who will then find their place within the existing social order. Services that were examples of this approach included the two Enabling Services commissioned in the large county authority we worked with focusing on services to disabled children. These services included an element of integration, in that they supported access to mainstream provision in the same way as the Gypsy/Traveller consortium sought to improve access to leisure services. However, the Enabling Services also aimed to promote and raise awareness and understanding about disabled children within those services that children accessed. The rationale was that by providing enabling support for a fixed period of time, confidence among families in mainstream provision could be built, but also that raising awareness within services would lead to inclusive services. The services relied on a bespoke approach to the work with both families and services, rather than a structured approach to the exclusion of disabled children from mainstream provision. That is, the starting point was particular services used by particular children rather than, for example, invoking the 1995 and 2005 Disability Discrimination Acts to secure broadly based inclusive services.

Separate provision

A rather different approach involved the development and support of separate provision for discrete targeted groups of children. Such services have restricted criteria for access and are highly focused. The groups targeted for such services are seen as having special needs, which result in their marginalisation. Specialist services are therefore needed to reduce this marginalisation so that it does not become destructive to the individuals concerned or to society. There were examples of this approach in services designed exclusively for disabled children, Gypsy/ Traveller children and some black and minority ethnic services.

The smaller of the two cities where we explored strategies for black and minority ethnic children supported two supplementary schools. The rationales for both schools highlighted the persistent failure to secure good outcomes within mainstream education for black and minority ethnic children and in particular those with African Caribbean heritage. Both schools targeted these groups and unlike mainstream schools were not open to all children from a particular geographical area or who met criteria linked to academic attainment and attendance. The schools provided an alternative curriculum to that taught in mainstream schools, for example history and literature studied was from the African and Asian continents with the explicit aim of countering the White-European focus of mainstream provision. The schools aimed to enable children to achieve good educational outcomes by raising their confidence through increased support with their academic work. As children achieved success in their supplementary studies, their confidence was raised and this confidence could be applied to their studies in mainstream settings. The schools also provided a greater amount of tutorial support than mainstream schools are able to do, offering high staff–student ratios and maintaining a focus of positively framing heritage and cultural traditions.

Working with community models

The fifth approach is one that offers a much less individualised perspective on prevention. This recognises the diversity of social life, draws on contextual knowledge of factors contributing to the processes of exclusion and builds on knowledge and understanding within communities to promote/enhance the capacity of children to reach their potential and reduce risks of exclusion. Building on strengths within family and community networks is seen as the first step towards enabling inclusion and effective participation in society. This approach was most evident in black and minority ethnic community-based services that adopt a social model of empowerment, and support for refugee and asylum-seeking groups that offer newly arrived families safe spaces to develop their networks.

A specific example comes from the London borough where we explored the preventative strategy for refugee and asylum-seeking children. The Parent and Community Network organisation grew from an initial meeting of parents from a particular refugee community concerned about the educational underachievement and involvement in crime and gang culture of their children and young people. Children and young people were included in this initial meeting and were invited to talk about their experiences and their suggestions for solutions to the emergent problems. An informal network of committed adults developed into a more formal group but without funding they were only able to offer homework support. Development support and funding from the Children's Fund enabled the formation of a formal organisation with associated policies and procedures. Adult and young members of the community worked together over time and the community-led nature of the initiative resulted in a range of provision being developed to support young people in education and study, but also a range of out-of-school provision providing positive activities. The organisation also targeted local agencies and organisations to raise awareness of their community and of the issues facing their young people. Over time, young people who had benefited from engaging with the project became volunteers and took on a range of formal roles and responsibilities.

Promoting well-being/achieving change

The final approach we identified was one that attempts to work with understandings about individual engagement and with understandings about achieving meaningful change in services and strategies. This is based on a recognition that existing services are limited in their capacity to address exclusionary processes and that the way they work can be potentially unhelpful for some groups of children. This approach also recognises that broader social relationships can be exclusionary. Thus, attempts to change children are set alongside broader work to challenge and reduce the barriers to inclusion facing children and families from within both services and communities.

This approach is illustrated by the Responsive Family Support project that worked with refugees and asylum seekers in a large city partnership. This service aimed to provide a responsive, multidimensional and holistic package of support for newly arrived families. Caseworkers undertook a strength-based assessment with the families referred and provided a range of individual supports for parents, children and young people, but also worked with the family as a unit. The project aimed to empower families by helping them achieve independence, and our evidence indicates considerable success in this regard. The project worked to link families with social and community networks that could offer support in the longer term. As well as providing support and services directly to families, the project signposted as appropriate and provided supported access to other services where necessary. The project also advocated for families within services and bureaucratic structures and delivered training across the city to raise awareness of newly arrived families and increase the capacity of mainstream and other services to work effectively with refugee children and families. By working in this way, families became more settled in their new communities and more confident in accessing services. But the barriers to inclusion were also challenged, with significant energies being directed at changing the services provided. These also seemed to be effective, for example the initial intensive support for schools was withdrawn as schools became confident in supporting newly arrived children.

Our analysis distinguishes the types of approach that were evident rather than defining individual partnerships. The strategies adopted by Children's Fund partnerships and the services provided combined elements of these approaches to different degrees. The emphasis placed on the different elements varied according to the commissioning process, the changing needs of children and families or the changing guidance provided locally and nationally. Some services sat tightly within one approach with highly focused responses; others demonstrated a capacity to incorporate a number of approaches. Table 1 summarises the approaches and the assumptions on which they are based.

In addition to the six types of approach to prevention, there was also evidence of localised and reactive planning that may or may not be underpinned by intentions linked to addressing wider issues of social exclusion. This approach focused on meeting the immediate and presenting needs within an area. External change initiatives (such as the Children's Fund) were seen in this approach as supplementary funding streams that would enable gaps in service provision to be filled. The service response was reactive – it responded to the various presenting needs of individuals or groups of children that were not being met by other existing services, and this cannot be considered to constitute a strategic approach in the way those detailed above appear to do so.

Table 1: Summary of approaches to prevention

Category	Intent – primary driver	Description of provision	Assumptions about relationship between child, community and society
Integration (changing child focus)	Integration into existing provision, which is functional and appropriate	Focus is on child's capabilities/capacities to engage with the existing provision	Social exclusion can be addressed without structural/cultural change
Adaptation (changing service focus)	Increasing the responsivity of the mainstream services	Focus is on enhancing existing provision	Increasing social cohesion requires greater diversity in service provision
Separated provision (child/their community focus)	Certain groups need bespoke services to avoid problematic outcomes	Highly focused and offered only to those meeting a specific criteria	Specialist services to ensure marginalisation does not become destructive
Working with community models (mixed focus on child and services)	Contextual knowledge building on community understandings	Developed by and reflects existing community models of help and support	Current social life is diverse and inclusion is achieved by building on networks
Promoting well-being/achieving change (mixed focus on child and services)	Mixed intent; promoting the child's potential and changing the services	Aims to provide a broad service tackling a range of barriers	Existing social organisation is not benign but child also needs to change to engage with enhanced provision

It is possible to see within the categories in Table 1, different emphases being placed on changing the child or changing social structures and relationships. Some of the approaches led to greater attention being given to the barriers to inclusion; others adopted a focus of changing the individual child's behaviour or experiences to enable inclusion. Services sometimes used more than one of these approaches and the evaluation identified services that, while focusing on integrating children, also, for example, built on community models. This analysis represents a development of Hardiker et al's earlier work. Their argument that thinking about prevention needs to be located in an understanding of different models of the welfare state is here extended to address contemporary assumptions about the nature of the relationship between children and their communities and where the responsibility for change lies. This new framework was developed from data that described the diversity of activity being undertaken in practice with children considered to be at risk of exclusion, and is therefore rooted in empirical evidence about contemporary provision.

The policy developments considered in Chapter Four, which mark a shift in thinking about child welfare from children at risk of harm to children at risk of social exclusion, have enabled new understandings of prevention to emerge. Table 1, which draws together the evidence from the evaluation of the Children's Fund with an analysis of the underpinning drivers, offers those developing policy and practice an opportunity to consider the links between their practical action and desired outcomes in relation to social exclusion/inclusion.

Next steps

The growing emphasis on highly targeted initiatives that has characterised the latter stages of New Labour's child and family policy suggests further implications for the way in which prevention is being conceptualised. Increasingly, the 'othering' of those failing to take up and engage with the generic preventative programmes suggests that a combined model of separate services but with some integrationist intentions is being promoted (see Table 1). The development of projects such as the multi-systemic therapy pilots and the family–nurse partnership scheme (SEU, 2007) is framed by a policy discourse that suggests that families perceived as high risk and failing require separate services but ones that implicitly or explicitly impose expectations of integration into the mainstream.

The evaluation of these targeted services (see, for example, Nixon et al, 2006) continues to suggest that a proportion of those intended users of the services fail to engage. As the government narrows the focus for the target groups for preventative initiatives, the prospect is that prevention will become increasingly coupled with enforcement, and that further developments of the conceptual frameworks will be required that build on the analysis offered by Tisdall (2006), Gillies (2005) and others, which locates prevention in a punitive context (see the discussion in Chapters Three and Four).

The analysis of the data from NECF revealed the extent to which exclusionary processes were addressed and identified new ways of categorising preventative approaches. However, while this analysis of existing activity aids understanding of contemporary approaches, it does not necessarily lead to the development of new frameworks that could support effective preventative strategies and practices. In Chapter Eight we consider how new approaches to prevention could be built, using both the conceptual understandings of social exclusion and the analysis of preventative services and practices contained within this chapter.

EIGHT

Conclusion: effective preventative approaches

Introduction

In this final chapter we draw together the analysis of the changing policy environment for prevention with our analysis emerging from the empirical data generated by the National Evaluation of the Children's Fund (NECF) to arrive at some suggestions as to how effective preventative policies and practices could be developed in the future. We begin by reviewing the key themes emerging from the previous chapters, and then consider the implications of these for conceptualising prevention. We go on to rehearse the domains that theory and evidence suggest we need to consider if preventative approaches are to be effective. We conclude by exploring how new approaches to prevention could be developed, and what these may look like in practice.

An overview of the key themes

Social exclusion

The preceding chapters have explored the dominance of social exclusion in the New Labour discourses concerned with children and families. While we have acknowledged that social exclusion is a contested concept, we have also suggested that it is a useful lens through which the experiences of marginalised children and families can be viewed. In particular, social exclusion allows the dynamic and multifaceted nature of these experiences to be understood. This book has explored the specific experiences of particular groups of children – who sit within families or communities that are perceived to be at significant risk of social exclusion and resultant poor outcomes in later life. But we have also recognised the broader experiences of children within the UK, in particular those who face the challenges of poverty and deprivation, and noted that their European counterparts fare considerably better. Adopting perspectives of exclusionary and inclusionary processes ensures that the multifaceted nature of marginalised children and families' lived experiences can be explored and responded to – however inadequately this may have occurred in policy and practice. We suggested that a set of domains can be identified as potentially exclusionary. These are:

- material dimensions;
- spatial exclusions;
- access to goods and services;
- health and well-being;
- cultural;
- self-determination;
- public decision making.

The extent to which preventative initiatives have been willing, or able, to address this range of domains has been questioned in the analysis we have provided within this book. Despite central government rhetoric, in reality the translation of policies concerned with social exclusion into grassroots services and practices has been argued to have resulted in a narrow focus for change – primarily that of individual capacity and engagement.

We have argued in the earlier chapters that the arrival of New Labour brought with it a rapidly changing policy landscape in child welfare. The bringing together of a range of economic and social projects with the intentions of producing economically and socially robust future citizens has underpinned developments in child welfare policies and practices. For children and families, the emphasis moved from individual assessments of need towards generic outcomes for all children. These outcomes sat within an understanding of social exclusion and its consequences, with some groups meriting particular attention. New Labour also brought to the fore the role of parents, and implicitly and explicitly sought to bind parents into a partnership with the state in working towards the production of economically and socially viable future citizens. The 'othering' of those who failed either to engage with the opportunities presented or to conform with mainstream notions of parenting enabled the development of punitive policies that sat alongside the raft of support-based initiatives (see, for example, the discussion of the Respect agenda in Chapter Three). All these developments have been the subject of critical analysis concerned with the disappearance of anti-poverty strategies at the point of service delivery to families where experiences of exclusionary processes was seemingly reinterpreted as the individual capacity to change and conform.

Prevention

In the preceding chapters we have traced the changing context for prevention in child welfare and we have reviewed the strengths and weaknesses of existing conceptual understandings of prevention. The historical models of individual interventions that aimed to prevent children from developing acute needs and requiring formal interventions have been replaced, we suggest, by approaches that are concerned with disrupting children's pathways into exclusion and promoting inclusionary experiences. We have argued that the tiered frameworks for prevention no longer meet the conceptual needs of contemporary preventative approaches. The tiered models adapted and used by policy makers and practitioners fail to capture the underlying intentions and assumptions about the exclusionary processes that are informing the preventative approach, and may simply be driven by service functionality. Also, our data revealed that often the complexities of need presented by children and families cannot sit within a single 'tier'; they may present a multitude of needs of varying intensity simultaneously. As a result, these traditional models fail to capture both the contemporary context for prevention – that of social exclusion and the scale and types of preventative needs – and understandings about how inclusion can be addressed.

Delivering preventative services

We have noted the changing arrangements for delivering services. In particular, attention has been paid to two themes – the rise of multi-agency working and the role of the third sector. The shifting focus of political attention in prevention has been accompanied by a series of policy steers and more recently legislative changes that have required local authorities to put in place increasingly integrated service arrangements and provision for children. The previous silos of mainstream providers were argued by New Labour to act as a barrier to effective support for children at risk of poor outcomes. The joining up of services with a shared generic set of outcomes was promoted as a necessary mechanism for achieving change for children. While the evidence may indicate that consequently much professional (and evaluatory) attention has been diverted into brokering professional relationships in this new framework (Sloper, 2004; Frost, 2005) rather than addressing the reasons for needs arising, the government has remained steadfastly committed to this theme of integration. Prevention and preventative services have proved to be fertile ground for taking forward this joined-up policy – various national preventative initiatives have piloted approaches to multi-agency working and the legal frameworks for children's services now dictate that such approaches should be adopted in designing and delivering prevention at a local level.

The role of the third sector has been at times a contradictory one in this new policy and practice landscape for prevention (NCVCCO, 2008). At times, the history and experience of the voluntary and community sector in developing and delivering prevention has been recognised and valued. But other developments have – on occasion almost simultaneously – rendered the third sector vulnerable and dependent on the goodwill and accessibility of local mainstream providers. While the voluntary sector can argue a long history in seeking to meet the needs of children and families at risk of social exclusion, its capacity to influence and inform statutory providers has waxed and waned. The relatively recent development of specific guidance for the involvement of the third sector in integrated children's services (DCSF, 2007) indicated both the political desire to explicitly commit to this sector and a recognition of the often tenuous working links that exist at local levels.

Learning from the data: conceptual frameworks

We have used the data from NCSF to provide an insight into how preventative approaches are being developed and implemented locally and nationally. We have suggested that the impact of this initiative on the dimensions of social exclusion has been limited. While we could see evidence of small-scale changes for individuals, we were unable to identify systemic change leading to the emergence of inclusionary processes and outcomes. However, the data do allow the approaches to prevention being adopted by strategic stakeholders and practitioners to be described. We have suggested that a typology of the approaches being adopted can be identified. These approaches reveal assumptions about the nature of social exclusion and the understandings held about the relationships between children, families and the state. While the data and the analysis did not find evidence of ways of working that generated significant change, it is possible to use the learning from the strengths and weaknesses of the preventative approaches adopted to begin to build new conceptual and practice frameworks that can address the multidimensional nature of social exclusion.

In Chapter Seven we were able to consider the data that described preventative activities against the dimensions of social exclusion described in Chapter Two. The evidence from NECF was that, although its overarching objective was concerned with poverty and exclusion, its implementation often resulted in a focus on the excluded rather than the excluding and neither the design nor the implementation of the initiative was capable of making a radical impact on current child poverty. Our analysis of the dimensions of social exclusion suggests that multifaceted approaches are needed that engage with different but interlinking spheres of personal and social life that are important to children and their families. These include:

- the relational networks within and across the neighbourhoods in which they live;
- the services that are designed or intended to support their development and meet their needs at times of difficulty;
- the personal and interpersonal sphere: children as active agents and impacted by others' relationships with them; and
- the political sphere, in which policy decisions are made that affect social justice.

This analysis of children and families existing and surviving within multiple, overlapping domains of difficulty is reflected by research elsewhere. Power (2007) suggests that families surviving urban deprivation engage with a series of 'levels' or layers – some of which are seen to offer support and some of which are perceived as hostile and inhibiting. She argues that six layers can be identified for what she describes as 'city survivors'. These layers are complex in their impact, and parents are argued to expend considerable time brokering the impact of the layers to enable children to grow and flourish. Often, neighbourhoods are perceived as hostile, but equally, community matters as a source of social contact and support. Parents perceive 'dangers' in their neighbourhood, but also carry a fear of the wider world. The picture revealed by Power's research is a complex one and echoes NECF findings, which suggested that a key impact of this large-scale preventative programme was to expose the extent and complexity of the needs of children and families in many different circumstances.

This conceptual framework of a complex network or spheres within which families experience inclusionary and exclusionary processes also has resonance with the literature exploring the significance of social and environmental networks. For example, Morrow (2004) has explored the way in which children conceptualise friendship and how friendship networks are important for children. This highlights their importance for children's sense of identity and belonging and the way in which the trust developed within these relationships is not generalisable to the wider community. Family and wider kin are also important, but formal community networks have much less relevance for children and young people. These findings resonate with evidence from NECF of the significance of relationships that children were able to establish with each other in the context of Children's Fund activities. In the context of work with refugee and asylum-seeking children, for example, the development of supportive and trusting relationships between children from different backgrounds was cited by children as a contributory factor in the benefits they experienced.

Network analysis has been applied to a number of social practices. For example, Folgheraiter (2007) uses the lens of relational social work to explore the role of networks in achieving change for children. He suggests that children's networks can be utilised as a resource for change. He proposes that professionals map networks and, through supporting those parts that are strong and effective, work with them to achieve better outcomes for children. While debates can be had about the 'screening' role of the professional in this approach, this is an example of a theoretically grounded approach to practice that emphasises not only the importance of understanding children's lives in the context of social relationships, but also of recognising that children's networks can be instrumental in change processes. Links can be made here to the uneven picture of participatory practices revealed by the analysis of NECF data, and the diversity in approaches that was evident in engaging children, families and their communities.

Links can also be made from the research and literature we have described to ecological approaches to child development and family experiences. Historically, this body of literature has been concerned with exploring the interrelationship between children's development and their surrounding environments (physically, emotionally and socially) (for example, Bronfenbrenner, 1979; Jack, 2000; Gill and Jack, 2007). This work has also informed the literature exploring the impact of community-based initiatives on family life and outcomes for children. Barnes et al (2006b) suggest that links to an ecological approach are evident in many of the community initiatives that they reviewed, and certainly such approaches are argued to be an underpinning theoretical framework for various national and local practice developments (see, for example, the Department for Health's *Framework for the Assessment of Children in Need and Their Families* [DH, 2000]). The evidence of the impact of such models and approaches is seen to be mixed – with some suggestion that it is unclear as to the extent to which community initiatives can achieve change in child-level outcomes:

> Overall, while community development is still an important aim in its own right, the jury is still out on whether it is sensible to direct resources to community development if one wants to enhance child development or prevent child abuse. It may be better to focus on the children or parents directly, albeit by providing accessible community based services. (Barnes et al, 2006b, p 131)

Our focus in considering the impact of the Children's Fund and the context within which it sat, has been the exclusionary and inclusionary processes that shape the experiences of children and families. We have tried to consider how prevention has been understood by policy makers and practitioners and what these understandings reveal about the multidimensional processes of social exclusion. As indicated above, there is a substantial body of literature and research exploring approaches to prevention that address specific dimensions of children and families' lived experiences. We have also been able to consider the links into existing relevant conceptual frameworks. But, the data that we have been able to analyse also suggest that the complexity of the exclusionary processes experienced by families remains relatively underrepresented in the actual services and practices developed.

Implementing new approaches

We have emphasised the complexity of the challenge that needs to be addressed if effective preventative strategies are to be implemented. We can suggest that responding adequately to this challenge requires adopting a number of principles.

Robust and varied data

In Chapter Five we considered the limits to the data available to identify need and determine which groups should be targeted for preventative action. The use of administrative data may neither address the exclusionary processes that families experience nor capture either their lived experiences or their perspectives on the services that they receive.

For example, Hughes and Fielding (2006) have argued the potential value of data that captures strengths and capacities, thereby allowing positive experiences to be built on. The data needed to support a more complex approach to prevention would require careful reflection and sophisticated analysis – something that rapidly changing policy contexts may not permit.

A multidimensional analysis of need

Our empirical evidence suggests that the linking together of existing strands of needs analysis was rare. For example, the experiences of African Caribbean boys within the local school as well as within their home, within the local healthcare services and within their community, was rarely drawn together, resulting in responses to need that were narrow or imbalanced. An analysis of needs that draws together the impact of different dimensions of social exclusion will necessitate communication across the different agencies working with these children and families and involve the families themselves.

Exclusionary analysis

The analysis of the data indicated that while assumptions about exclusionary processes may be apparent in the activities supported, explicit analytical statements of the exclusionary process impacting the well-being of children and families were absent. Debates occurred about who to target, and at what level – debates that are echoed in empirical evidence from other prevention-focused evaluations (see, for example, reports from the national evaluation of Sure Start [NESS, 2005] and On Track [Dinos et al, 2006]). But there was little evidence of a focus on barriers to inclusion and thus on how strategies might target these rather than those who experience the negative effects of these barriers or processes.

Multiple collaborators

While we have acknowledged the preoccupation with multi-agency partnerships in prevention – sometimes to the detriment of resolving child and family needs – any multidimensional approach must engage the full range of collaborators, and evidence is clear that this should include the child, family and key members of significant networks – both within the locality and among relevant identity communities. Our evidence revealed the ambivalence of some parents to taking an active part in service planning and the value to them of services that offer some respite. Thus, precisely what 'participation' means has to be negotiated in specific contexts rather than imposed as another hoop through which families have to jump in order to receive help. The process of collaboration needs to be capable not only of engaging with families' lived experiences (see below), but also of understanding the way in which they work out what is right for them in terms of their responsibilities to each other. That is, working collaboratively with parents and children requires a value-based approach that offers recognition and respect as well as practical help.

The other aspect of collaboration that our work has highlighted is that between statutory and third sector agencies. In this context, collaboration should not mean passing over responsibility to voluntary and community agencies to deliver on the prevention agenda without being prepared to make changes in the way in which the statutory sector operates. The need for two-way learning and support is highlighted by the Children's Fund experience.

Multifaceted preventative strategies

Collaboration across agencies, groups and individuals working directly with children and families also needs to be embedded within other initiatives and strategies that are designed to improve well-being, regenerate communities and counter social exclusion. At the time of the Children's Fund these included, for example, the New Deal for Communities and the development of neighbourhood management schemes. At the time of writing, the White Paper *Communities in Control: Real Power, Real People* (DCLG, 2008) was proposing initiatives such as a community builders scheme to help local community groups thrive and programmes designed to encourage young people to get more involved in their local communities. The speed of policy change makes it hard for initiatives to link up at a local level and current uncertainty about the future of New Labour in government may mean that future policy directions are even harder to predict. But our analysis emphasises the necessity for multifaceted approaches that impact the multiple forces that contribute to social exclusion. This multidimensional approach may be better achieved through developing synergies with other initiatives.

Explicit linking to lived experiences

Data from NECF and elsewhere indicate that children and families value responsive, flexible services rooted in trustworthy relationships. The Children's Fund evidence also indicates that it is unsafe to make assumptions about how children, families and communities will engage with provision. However, despite the reflections on services and practices emerging from service user evaluations of provision, there is a scarcity of data about the lived experiences of the families that are the focus of many New Labour preventative policies (Levitas et al, 2007; Morris et al, 2007). The works of Ridge (2002) and Power (2007) are exceptions. The development of research that increases understanding of the lived experiences of marginalised families will assist significantly in the advancement of preventative policies and practices.

The implications for existing preventative approaches

Our review can be seen to lead naturally to consideration of preventative approaches that address the exclusionary processes within the domains identified, while simultaneously responding to the evidence from children and families about the valued components of existing approaches. Such approaches would need to move beyond responding to specific types of need or limited aspects of children and families' lived experiences. Instead, preventative strategies and practices would need to rest on a multidimensional analysis that requires fresh approaches to the conceptualisation and mapping of need.

There are substantial implications within this analysis for the paradigm of risk-based prevention. Initiatives that are developed within a risk and protective factors paradigm focus on the identified domains of 'family', 'school', 'community' and 'personal' risk factors, with protective factors commonly understood to be the converse, or absence of risk in these domains. The 'school' and 'community' domains have potential for the recognition of contextual or structural factors impacting on the child or young person. But what this means for policy interventions and practice is undeveloped; as our analysis shows, the focus remains on building children's individual resilience or ability to overcome the risk factors that they face. For example, growing up in a disadvantaged community is identified as a key risk factor in policy discourse, but interventions for young people identified as presenting or experiencing risk hold limited capacity to engage with changes to their community, or to the services that do (or do not) operate in the area. This may simply be the absence of joined-up initiatives, but may also reflect an ongoing emphasis on individual change and attainment. Interventions focus on providing activities that take the young person away from the perceived risk posed by their peers and their environment and equipping them with strategies to resist risky behaviour and the risks judged as inherent in their community. Where the community context is addressed more directly the initiatives and services developed target individuals and families within those neighbourhoods to change their behaviours and build the resilience that they are seen to lack (for example, initiatives such as On Track: Finch et al, 2006; or Communities that Care: Crow et al, 2004). As a result, attempts to develop holistic and multifaceted approaches remain within the narrow paradigm of 'risk and protection', resulting in a focus on individual resilience.

A recent review for the Youth Justice Board (Mason and Prior, 2008) sought to identify techniques for ensuring that young people are engaged in the programmes that are designed to reduce their offending. It concluded that referral to initiatives identified as effective is not enough in itself; young people require ongoing, individualised casework support that includes advocacy and brokerage of access to services and provision. It also highlighted the need for local, inclusive provision to be developed so that young people at risk can access the services that are so often lacking in availability. The review concluded that working with young people in isolation from the context around them (within a risk and protective factors framework) is unlikely to achieve change.

From the research explored here, the closest example we can identify to the framework that we present in this chapter is the Responsive Family Support service for refugee and asylum-seeking families that we discussed in Chapter Six. The service aimed to be responsive to families' needs, and to the needs of individuals within them, but also aimed to change structural and service contexts –for example changing the capacity of schools as they gained experience of working with newly arrived families. The following sections illustrate how this service addressed the key dimensions we have identified.

Robust and varied data

The service did not rely on administrative data to identify families. Referrals came from a variety of routes including self-referral. A strengths-based assessment sought to build on strengths and capacities within the family as well as address needs, and detailed case files containing a wealth of data were maintained and used to develop indicators of success across a range of domains and which could capture qualitative evidence to demonstrate change. This time-consuming process was recognised as necessary by the services managers and commissioners, who supported them in the process.

Multidimensional analysis of need

The service sought to work with families in a holistic and responsive way. To this end, no areas of families lives were excluded by the service and families were encouraged to be open about all aspects of their lives and experience. Caseworkers sought to broker support from other agencies, advocate on families' behalf, and were careful to be honest about the limits to the areas they could address directly as a service and the limits to their expertise. This preparedness to make connections across service boundaries was particularly valued by families. Where an area was outside of their remit or knowledge, caseworkers ensured that families were signposted to other provision and that their access was supported. The service was based on dedicated caseworkers providing a package of support, for as long as was required, through a mix of direct provision and supported access.

Exclusionary analysis

Caseworkers focused on the exclusionary processes and factors that they and families identified within other agencies, organisations and provision. Caseworkers advocated within these structures, but also sought to change them through awareness-raising training, through targeted resources that explained statutory duties or the implications of legislation and through the active membership of forums and strategic mechanisms so that work was constantly taking place to challenge and change barriers to inclusion.

Multiple collaborators

As indicated above, the service worked to develop multiple partnerships with statutory, voluntary and private sector organisations to provide holistic responsive support. It was supported by the local authority and contributed learning to schools and other agencies about ways of working that were effective in supporting refugee and asylum-seeking children and families. The identification and response to families' needs were negotiated with them.

Multifaceted prevention strategies

As well as working to meet the needs of families and individuals within them, the service worked with partners to ensure that need for its specialised provision was reduced. Examples include work with schools to develop their capacity so that their need for support was reduced.

Explicit linking to lived experiences

Children, young people and families valued the responsive service and the trusting relationships built with caseworkers. They contrasted the service with others that they had been in contact with and which had failed to work with them in the same respectful way, which they identified as being based within empathy, understanding and trusting relationships.

Such an example starts to indicate the complexity and scale of the preventative approach being proposed in this concluding chapter. In this example there are indications of altered approaches to mapping needs, monitoring impact, forming partnerships and the emphasis of the strategies and practices. While recognising the scale and significance of the changes to existing approaches, we argue that without these changes the capacity for existing models and approaches to effect long-term change will be limited.

Looking ahead

The context for this book has been the policies and initiatives of the New Labour government (within a broader history of approaches to child welfare). Our analysis of approaches to prevention, our proposed new understandings of prevention and the implications of these for policy and practice stem from our research within a time where New Labour has dominated government. Yet, despite this stability of office, we have seen how policy for children, young people and families has been subject to the flux and change that has characterised its longer history.

Although we locate much of our discussion within the current context of Every Child Matters and the future implications we can identify as stemming from this, our analysis should not be seen as limited to this context. We argue that any policy framework concerned with practice with children, young people and families needs to address prevention within the broader and complex experiences of social exclusion. With this in mind, it is perhaps worth briefly considering what is emerging about the Conservative plans for tackling the disadvantages and difficulties faced by children and their families.

The Centre for Social Justice was commissioned by David Cameron, as Conservative Party leader, to establish a Social Justice Policy Group (SJPG) to make policy recommendations to the Conservative Party (SJPG, 2006). The SJPG has identified five pathways to poverty (although it is not clear how): family breakdown, educational failure, economic dependence, indebtedness and addictions (SJPG, 2006, p 13). The SJPG (2006, p 18) states that, in contrast to previous Conservative Party policies, 'it cannot be acceptable for us to ignore the concept of relative poverty and social exclusion'. It also proposes 'much more early intervention and support for children and families' (SJPG, 2007a, p 7) and recognises 'the immense potential of smaller [third sector organisations] to play a large role in tackling poverty, especially through their preventative work' (SJPG, 2007b, p 5). However, there is no indication that an understanding of social exclusion is linked to a structural and multidimensional analysis such as we have presented as necessary for preventative action. Indeed, prevention is framed in terms of preventing reliance on welfare benefits, preventing the breakdown of the family and preventing the problems that are identified as resulting from this breakdown and its association with poverty (SJPG, 2007c). Thus, although there are indications of an intention to address social exclusion through early intervention, there is little indication that the policy frameworks proposed will be configured in the way that we suggest in our analysis here. It is clearly of limited value to comment in detail on the future possible developments within the UK government – but it is evident that the concepts described in this book will remain part of the political agenda for children and families.

Conclusion

We have argued, using empirical data and analyses of policy and provision, that new conceptual understandings of prevention are required if the challenge of reducing the social exclusion experienced by children and their families is to be realised. We have suggested that the effectiveness of preventative strategies and practices rests on a complex multidimensional analysis of needs and provision. But we are also aware, as the preceding example of the Responsive Family Support service shows, that such developments demand the resources to support new practices. As we have recognised in Chapters Three and Four, many current UK preventative programmes secured relatively short-term funding within a framework of unwieldy and unresponsive performance indicators. It is therefore insufficient to ask local policy makers and practitioners to change their activities. Wider changes in funding and in the chosen frameworks for outcomes are also required. Existing frameworks – such as the Every Child Matters outcomes set out in Chapter Four – maintain a focus on individual attainment, making the complex approach proposed in this chapter difficult to promote. However, without such changes, the risk is that preventative strategies and practices will continue to be separated from the broader exclusionary and inclusionary processes that ultimately determine the lived experiences of children and their families.

References

Ahmed, S. (2004) *Preventative Services for Black and Minority Ethnic Group Children and Families: A Review of Recent Literature*, Birmingham: NECF, www.ne-cf.org

Aldgate, J. and Tunstill, J. (1995) *Section 17: The First 18 Months*, London: HMSO.

Audit Commission (2000) *A New City: Supporting Asylum Seekers and Refugees in London*, London: Audit Commission.

Barnes, J., Katz, I., Korbin, K. and O'Brien, M. (2006) *Children and Families in Communities: Theory, Research, Policy and Practice*, Chichester: Wiley.

Barnes, M. (1997) *Care, Communities and Citizens*, Harlow: Addison Wesley, Longman.

Barnes, M. and Morris, K. (2008) 'Strategies for the prevention of social exclusion: an analysis of the Children's Fund', *Journal of Social Policy*, vol 35, no 2, pp 251-70.

Barnes, M., Sullivan, H. and Matka, E. (2001) *Context, Strategy and Capacity: Initial Findings from the Strategic Level Analysis*, Case study report for Lambeth, Southwark and Lewisham Health Action Zone, June, Birmingham: University of Birmingham.

Barnes, M., Sullivan, H. and Matka, E. (2003) *The Development of Collaborative Capacity in Health Action Zones: A Final Report from the National Evaluation*, Birmingham: University of Birmingham.

Barnes, M., Bauld, L., Benzeval, M., Judge, K., Mackenzie, M. and Sullivan, H. (2005) *Health Action Zones: Partnerships for Health Equity*, London: Routledge.

Barnes, M., Evans, R., Plumridge, G. and McCabe, A. (2006) *Preventative Services for Disabled Children: A Final Report of the National Evaluation of the Children's Fund*, London: DfES.

Batsleer, J. and Humphries, B. (eds) (2000) *Welfare, Exclusion and Political Agency*, London: Routledge.

BBC (British Broadcasting Corporation) (2007) 'UK is accused of failing children', 14 February, http://news.bbc.co.uk/1/hi/uk/6359363.stm

Bebbington, A. and Miles, J. (1989) 'The background of children who enter local authority care', *British Journal of Social Work*, vol 19, no 5, pp 349-68.

Beirens, H., Hughes, N., Hek, R. and Spicer, N. (2007) 'Preventing social exclusion of refugee and asylum seeking children: building new networks', *Social Policy and Society*, vol 6, no 2, pp 219-29.

Beirens, H., Hughes, N., Mason, P. and Spicer, N. (2006) *Preventative Services for Asylum seeking Children: A Final review of the National Evaluation of the Children's Fund*, London: DfES.

Benard, B. (1991) *Fostering Resiliency in Kids: Protective Factors in the Family, School and Community*, Portland, OR: Western Center for Drug-Free Schools and Communities.

Berghman, J. (1995) 'Social exclusion in Europe: policy context and analytical framework', in G. Room (ed) *Beyond the Threshold: The Measurement and Analysis of Social Exclusion*, Bristol: The Policy Press.

Billings, J., Dixcon, J., Mijanovich, T. and Wennberg, D. (2006) 'A method of predicting individual patients at highest risk of readmission to hospital in the next 12 months'. *British Medical Journal*, vol 333, no 756, p 327.

Blair, M. (2001) *Why Pick on Me? School Exclusion and Black Youth*, Stoke-on-Trent: Trentham Books.

Blair, T. (2006) 'Our nation's future – social exclusion', Speech given on 5 September, http://www.number10.gov.uk/Page10037

Bradshaw, J., Finch, N., Mayhew, E., Ritakallio, V.-M. and Skinner, C. (2006) *Child Poverty in Large Families*, Bristol: The Policy Press.

Bronfenbrenner, U. (1979) *The Ecology of Human Development: Experiments by Nature and Design*, Cambridge, MA: Harvard University Press.

Burnett, R. and Appleton, C. (2004) 'Joined-up services to tackle youth crime', *British Journal of Criminology*, vol 44, no 1, pp 34-54.

Byrne, D. (1999) *Social Exclusion*, Buckingham: Open University Press.

Clarke, H. (2006) *Preventing Social Exclusion of Disabled Children and their Families*, DfES Research Report 782 (produced for the National Evaluation of the Children's Fund), London: DfES.

Connell, J.P. and Kubisch, A.C. (eds) (1998) 'Applying a theory of change approach to the evaluation of comprehensive community initiatives: progress, prospects and problems', in K. Fulbright-Anderson, A.C. Kubisch and J.P. Connell (eds) *New Approaches to Evaluating Community Initiatives Volume 2: Theory, Measurement and Analysis* (pp 15-44), Washington, DC: The Aspen Institute.

Coote, A., Allen, J. and Woodhead, D. (2004) *Finding Out What Works: Understanding Complex, Community-Based Initiatives*, London: The King's Fund.

Crow, I., France, A., Hacking, S. and Hart, M. (2004) *Does Communities that Care Work? An Evaluation of a Community-Based Risk Prevention Programme in Three Neighbourhoods*, York: York Publishing.

CYPU (Children and Young People's Unit) (2001a) *Tomorrow's Future: Building a Strategy for Children and Young People*, London: DfES.

CYPU (2001b) *The Children's Fund Guidance*, London: DfES.

Davis, J. and Watson, N. (2001) 'Where are the children's experiences? Analysing social and cultural exclusion in "special" and "mainstream" schools', *Disability & Society*, vol 16, no 5, pp 671-87.

DCLG (Department for Communities and Local Government (2008) *Communities in Control: Real Power, Real People*, White Paper, London: DCLG.

DCSF (Department for Children, Schools and Families) (2007a) *The Children's Plan: Building Brighter Futures*, London: DCSF.

DCSF (2007b) *Third Sector Strategy and Action Plan*, Nottingham: DfES Publications.

DfES (Department for Education and Skills) (2003a) *Aiming High: Raising the Achievement of Minority Ethnic Pupils*, London: DfES.

DfES (2003b) *Every Child Matters*, London: DfES.

DfES (2004a) *Every Child Matters: Change for Children*, London: DfES.

DfES (2004b) *Every Child Matters: The Next Steps*, London: DfES.

DfES (2005) *Every Child Matters Outcomes Framework*, London: DfES, www.everychildmatters.gov.uk

DfES (2006) *Youth Matters: The Next Steps*, London: DfES.

DH (Department of Health) (1991) *Patterns and Outcomes in Child Placement*, London: HMSO.

DH (1995) *Child Protection: Messages from Research*, London: HMSO.

DH (2000) *Framework for the Assessment of Children in Need and Their Families*, London: The Stationery Office.

DH (2001) *The Children Act Now: Messages From Research*, London: HMSO.

DH (2002) *Learning From Past Experience: A Review of Serious Case Reviews*, London: HMSO.

Dinos, S., Tian, Y. and Solanki, A.-R. with Huari, H. (2006) *National Evaluation of On Track Phase Two: Tracking Services and Users: On Track in Practice*, Nottingham: DfES Publications.

Dobson, B. and Middleton, S. (1998) *Paying to Care: The Cost of Childhood Disability*, York: JRF.

Dorling, D., Rigby, J., Wheeler, B., Ballas, D., Thomas, B., Fahmy, E., Gordon, D. and Lupton, R. (2007) *Poverty, Wealth and Place in Britain, 1968 to 2005*, York: JRF.

DWP (Department for Work and Pensions) (2006) *Opportunity for All: Eight Annual Report 2006 Strategy Document*, London: DWP.

DWP (2007a) *Households Below Average Income (HBAI) 1994/5-2005/6 (Revised)*, www.dwp.gov.uk/asd/hbai/hbai2006/contents.asp

DWP (2007b) *Working for Children*, London: DWP.

Edwards, A., Barnes, M., Plewis, I. and Morris, K. (2006) *Working to Prevent the Social Exclusion of Children and Young People: Final Lessons from the National Evaluation of the Children's Fund*, DfES Research Report 734, London: DfES.

European Commission (1993) *European Social Policy Options for the Union*, Green Paper, COM (93) 551, Brussels: European Commission.

Evans, R. and Spicer, N. (2008) 'Is participation prevention?: a blurring of discourses in children's preventative initiatives in the UK', *Childhood*, vol 15, no 1, pp 50-73.

Farrington, D. (1996) *Understanding and Preventing Youth Crime*, York: JRF.

Farrington, D. (2000) 'Explaining and preventing crime: the globalisation of knowledge. Key note address to the American society for criminology, 1999', *Criminology*, vol 38, no 1, pp 1-24.

Fawcett, B., Featherstone, F. and Goddard, J. (2004) *Contemporary Child Care Policy and Practice*, Basingstoke: Palgrave Macmillan.

Featherstone, B. (2006) 'Rethinking family support in the current policy context', *British Journal of Social Work*, vol 36, no 1, pp 5-19.

Featherstone, B., Rivett, M. and Scourfield, J. (2007) *Working with Men in Health and Social Care*, London: Sage Publications.

Feinstein, L. and Sabates, R. (2006) *Predicting Adult Life Outcomes from Earlier Signals: Identifying Those at Risk*, Report for the Prime Minister's Strategy Unit, London: Institute of Education, University of London.

Fernando, S. (1991) *Mental Health, Race and Culture*, Basingstoke: Macmillan.

Finch, S., Aye Maung, N., Jones, A., Tipping, S., Blom, A. and Ghate, D. (2006) *The National Evaluation of On Track Phase Two: Interim Findings from the First Wave of the Longitudinal Cohort Study*, London: DfES.

Folgheraiter, F. (2007) 'Social work: principles and practices', *Social Policy & Society*, vol 6, no 2, pp 265-74.

Fox-Harding, L. (1997) *Perspectives in Child Care Policy*, London: Longman.

France, A. (2008) 'Risk factor analysis and the youth question', *Journal of Youth Studies*, vol 11, no 1, pp 1-15.

France, A. and Utting, D. (2005) 'The paradigm of "risk and protection-focused prevention" and its impact on services for children and families', *Children & Society*, vol 19, no 2, pp 77-90.

Frost, N. (2005) *Child Welfare: Major Themes in Health and Social Welfare*, London: Routledge.

Gibbons, J., Conroy, S. and Bell, C. (1995) *Operating the Child Protection System*, London: HMSO.

Giddens, A. (1998) *The Third Way: The Renewal of Social Democracy*, Cambridge: Polity Press.

Gill, O. and Jack, G. (2007) *Child and Family in Context: Developing Ecological Practice in Disadvantaged Communities*, Lyme Regis: Russell House Publishing.

Gillies, V. (2005) 'Meeting parents' needs? Discourses of "support" and "inclusion" in family policy', *Critical Social Policy*, vol 25, no 1, pp 70-90.

Glass, N. (1999) 'Sure Start: the development of an early intervention programme for young children in the United Kingdom', *Children & Society*, vol 13, no 4, pp 257-64.

Goldson, B. and Muncie, J. (2006) 'Editors' introduction', in B. Goldson and J. Muncie (eds) *Youth Crime and Justice*, London: Sage Publications.

Gordon, D., Parker, R. and Loughran, F. with Heslop, P. (2000) *Disabled Children in Britain*, London: The Stationery Office.

Haines, K. and Drakeford, M. (1998) *Young People and Youth Justice*, Basingstoke: Macmillan.

Hansen, K. and Plewis, I. (2004) *Children at Risk: How Evidence from British Cohort Data Can Inform the Debate on Prevention*, London: Institute of Education, University of London and National Evaluation of the Children's Fund.

Hardiker, P., Exton, K. and Barker, M. (1989) 'The social policy contexts of prevention in child care', *British Journal of Social Work*, vol 21, pp 341-59.

Hardiker, P., Exton, K. and Barker, M. (1991) *Policies and Practices in Preventative Child Care*, Aldershot: Ashgate.

Harker, L. (2006) *Delivering on Child Poverty: What Would it Take? A Report for the Department for Work and Pensions*, London: DWP

Haynes, P. (2003) *Managing Complexity in the Public Services*, Marlow: Open University Press, McGraw-Hill.

Hek, R. (2005) *The Experiences and Needs of Refugee and Asylum Seeking Children in the UK: A Literature Review*, DfES Research Report 635, London: DfES.

Hester, R. (2004) *Services Provided to Gypsy Traveller Children: A Review of the Current Literature for the National Evaluation of the Children's Fund*, London: NECF.

Hirsch, D. (2006) *What Will It Take to End Child Poverty? Firing on All Cylinders*, York: JRF.

Hirsch, D. (2007) *Experiences of Poverty and Educational Disadvantage: Round-Up: Reviewing the Evidence*, York: JRF.

Home Office (1999) *Supporting Families: A Consultation Document*, London: HMSO.

Hughes, N. and Fielding, A. (2006) *Targeting Preventative Services for Children: Experiences from the Children's Fund*, DfES Research Report 777, London: DfES.

Hughes, N., Mason, P. and Prior, D. (2007) 'The socialisation of crime policy? Evidence from the National Evaluation of the Children's Fund', Papers from the Criminal Justice and Social Justice Conference, King's College, London, July.

Jack, G. (2000) 'Ecological influences on parenting and child development', *British Journal of Social Work*, vol 30, no 6, pp 703-20.

Jordan, B. (1996) *A Theory of Poverty and Social Exclusion*, Cambridge: Polity Press.

Jordan, B. (1998) *The New Politics of Welfare*, London: Sage Publications.

JRF (Joseph Rowntree Foundation) (2008) Child poverty project updates: June 2008, www.jrf.org.uk/child-poverty/updates.asp

Kiddle, C. (1999) *Traveller Children: A Voice for Themselves*, London: Jessica Kingsley Publishers.

King's Fund (2006) *Wanless Social Care Review: Securing Good Care for Older People: Taking a Long-Term View*, London: King's Fund.

Krumer-Nevo, M. (2003) 'From "a coalition of despair" to "a covenant of help" in social work with families in distress', *European Journal of Social Work*, vol 6, no 3, pp 273-82.

Lee, P. and Murie, A. (1999) 'Spatial and social divisions within British cities: beyond residualisation', *Housing Studies*, vol 14, no 5, pp 625-40.

Levitas, R. (2005) *The Inclusive Society? Social Exclusion and New Labour*, Basingstoke: Palgrave.

Levitas, R., Pantazis, C., Fahmy, E., Gordon, D., Lloyd, E. and Patsios, D. (2007) *The Multi-Dimensional Analysis of Social Exclusion*, London: Cabinet Office.

Lewis, P. (1994) *Islamic Britain: Religion, Politics and Identity among British Muslims*, London: I.B. Tauris.

Lindley, B. (1994) *On the Receiving End: Families' Experiences of the Court Process in Care and Supervision Proceedings under the Children Act 1989: Final Report*, London: Family Rights Group.

Lister, R. (2003) 'Investing in the citizen workers of the future: transformations in citizenship and the state under New Labour', *Social Policy and Administration*, vol 35, no 5, pp 427-43.

Lister, R. (2006) 'Children (but not women) first: New Labour, child welfare and gender', *Critical Social Policy*, vol 26, no 2, pp 315-35.

Little, M., Morpeth, L. and Axford, N. (2003) 'Children's services in the UK 1997-2003: problems, developments and challenges for the future', *Children & Society*, vol 17, no 3, pp 205-14.

MacMillan, J. and Brown, S. (1998) 'In whose interests? Politics and policy', in S. Brown (ed) *Understanding Youth Crime: Listening to Youth?*, Buckingham: Open University Press.

Macpherson, W. (1999) *The Stephen Lawrence Inquiry*, Cm 4262-1, London: The Stationery Office.

Marsh, P. and Crow, G. (1998) *Family Group Conferences in Child Welfare*, Oxford: Blackwell Science.

Mason, P. and Barnes, M. (2007) 'Constructing theories of change: methods and sources', *Evaluation*, vol 13, no 2, pp 151-70.

Mason, P. and Prior, D. (2008) 'The Children's Fund and the prevention of crime and anti-social behaviour', *Criminology and Criminal Justice*, vol 8, no 3, pp 279-316.

Mason, P., Farrow, K. and Prior, D. (forthcoming) *Access to Justice for Vulnerable Groups: Age*, London: Ministry of Justice.

Mason, P., Barnes, M., Plumridge, G., Beirens, H. and Broughton, K. (2006) *Preventative Services for Gypsy/Traveller Children: A Final Report of the National Evaluation of the Children's Fund*, London: DfES.

McGuire, J. (2002) 'Integrating findings from research reviews', in J. McGuire (ed) *Offender Rehabilitation and Treatment: Effective Programmes and Policies to Reduce Re-Offending*, Chichester: John Wiley.

Morris, K. (2004) 'Partnership working: changing understandings in child welfare services in England', *Protecting Children*, vol 19, no 2, pp 61-8.

Morris, K. (ed) (2008) *Social Work and Multi-agency Working: Making A Difference*, Bristol: The Policy Press.

Morris, K. and Barnes, M. (2008) 'Prevention and social exclusion: new understandings for policy and practice', *British Journal of Social Work*, vol 36, no 6, pp 1194-211.

Morris, K. and Burford, G. (2006) 'Working with children's networks: building opportunities for change?', *Social Policy and Society*, vol 6, no 2, pp 209-17.

Morris, K. and Spicer, N. (2003) *The National Evaluation of the Children's Fund: Emerging Messages for Practice*, London: DfES.

Morris, K., Warren, S., Plumridge, G. and Hek, R. (2006) *Preventative Services for Black and Minority Ethnic Children: A Final Report of the National Evaluation of the Children's Fund*, London: DfES.

Morris, K., Hughes, N., Clarke, H., Tew, J., Mason, P., Galvani, S., Lewis, A. and Lovelen, L. with Becker, S. and Burford, G. (2007) *Think Family: A Literature Review of Whole Family Approaches*, London: Cabinet Office.

Morrow, V. (2002) 'Children's accounts of friendship, family and place', in Muncie, J., Hughes, G. and McLaughlin, E. (2002) *Youth Justice: Critical Readings*, London: Sage Publications.

Muncie, J., Hughes, G. and McLaughlin, E. (eds) (2002) *Youth Justice: Critical Readings*, London: Sage.

National Evaluation of Sure Start Research Team (2005) *Early Impacts of Sure Start Local Programmes on Children and Families*, Report 13, London: DfES.

NCVCCO (National Council of Voluntary Child Care Organisations) (2008) *Under the Radar: A Survey of Small Organisations Working with Children, Young People and Families*, London: NCVCCO.

NECF (National Evaluation of the Children's Fund) (2003a) *Developing Collaboration in Preventative Services for Children and Young People: First Annual Report*, DfES Research Report 528, London: DfES.

NECF (2003b) *Early Messages for Developing Practice*, London: DfES.

NECF (2004) *Prevention and Early Intervention in the Social Inclusion of Children and Young People*, London: DfES.

NESS (National Evaluation of Sure Start) (2005) *Implementing Sure Start Local Programmes: An Integrated Overview of the First Four Years*, London: DfES.

Newman, T. (2002) *Promoting Resilience: A Review of Effective Strategies for Child Care Services*, Exeter: Centre for Evidence-Based Social Services, University of Exeter and Barnardo's.

Niner, P.M. (2005) *West Midlands Regional Housing Strategy, West Midlands Regional Spatial Strategy, Shared Evidence Base: Gypsies and Travellers*, Birmingham: School of Public Policy, University of Birmingham.

Nixon, J., Hunter, C., Parr, S., Myers, S., Whittle, S. and Sanderson, D. (2006) *Anti-Social Behaviour Intensive Family Support Projects: An Evaluation of Six Pioneering Projects*, London: ODPM.

O'Connor, W. and Lewis, J. (1999) *Experiences of Social Exclusion in Scotland: A Qualititative Research Study*, London: National Centre for Social Research.

Ofsted (Office for Standards in Education) (1996) *Exclusions from Secondary Schools*, London: HMSO.

Olds, D.I. (2006) 'The nurse–family partnership: an evidence-based preventive intervention', *Infant Mental Health Journal*, vol 27, no 1, pp 5-25.

Olsen, R. and Clarke, H. (2003) *Parenting and Disability: Disabled Parents' Experiences of Raising Children*, Bristol: The Policy Press.

Palmer, G., MacInnes, T. and Kenway, P. (2006) *Monitoring Poverty and Social Exclusion 2006*, York: JRF.

Parton, N. (1991) *Governing the Family: Child Care, Child Protection and the State*, London: Macmillan.

Parton, N. (ed) (1997) *Child Protection and Family Support: Tensions, Contradictions and Possibilities*, London: Routledge.

Parton, N. (2006) *Safeguarding Childhood: Early Intervention and Surveillance in a Late Modern Society*, Basingstoke: Palgrave Macmillan.

Percy-Smith, J. (ed) (2000) *Policy Responses to Social Exclusion: Towards Inclusion?*, Buckingham: Open University Press.

Pitts, J. (2001) 'The new correctionalism: young people, youth justice and New Labour', in R. Matthews and J. Pitts (eds) *Crime, Disorder and Community Safety*, London: Routledge.

Power, A. (2007) *City Survivors: Bringing Up Children in Disadvantaged Neighbourhoods*, Bristol: The Policy Press.

Priestley, M. (1999) *Disability Politics and Community Care*, London: Jessica Kingsley Publishers.

Prior, D. (2005) 'Evaluating the new youth justice: what can practitioners learn from research?', *Practice*, vol 17, no 2, pp 103-12.

Prior, D. and Paris, A. (2005) *Preventing Children's Involvement in Crime and Antisocial Behaviour: A Literature Review*, London: DfES.

Prior, D., Mason, P., Coad, J., Beirens, H. and McCutcheon, M. (2006) *The Children's Fund and Children and Young People at Risk of Crime and Anti-Social Behaviour*, Birmingham: NECF, www.ne-cf.org

Purdy, M. and Banks, D. (eds) (1999) *Health and Exclusion*, London: Routledge.

Reay, D. and Mirza, H.S. (1997) 'Uncovering the genealogies of the margins: black supplementary schooling', *British Journal of Sociology of Education*, vol 18, no 4, pp 477-99.

Respect Task Force (2007) *Respect Action Plan*, London: Home Office.

Ridge, T. (2002) *Childhood Poverty and Social Exclusion: From a Child's Perspective*, Bristol: The Policy Press.

Rose, W. (1994) Address to the Sieff Conference, 5 September.

Ryan, M. (2005) 'Engaging with punitive attitudes towards crime and punishment: some strategic lessons from England and Wales', in J. Pratt, D. Brown, M. Brown, S. Hallsworth and W. Morrison (eds) *The New Punitiveness*, Cullompton: Willan Publishing.

Sales, R. (2002) 'The deserving and undeserving? Refugees, asylum-seekers and welfare in Britain', *Critical Social Policy*, vol 22, no 3, pp 456-78.

Sayce, L. (2000) *From Psychiatric Patient to Citizen: Overcoming Discrimination and Social Exclusion*, Basingstoke: Macmillan.

Schoon, I. and Bynner, J. (2003) 'Risk and resilience in the life course: implications for interventions and social policies', *Journal of Youth Studies*, vol 6, no 1, pp 21-31.

SEU (Social Exclusion Unit) (1998a) *Truancy and Social Exclusion*, London: Jessica Kingsley Publishers.

SEU (1998b) *Bringing Britain Together: A National Strategy for Neighbourhood Renewal*, London: The Stationery Office.

SEU (2000) *National Strategy for Neighbourhood Renewal: Report of Policy Action Team 12: Young People*, London: SEU.

SEU (2006) *Reaching Out: An Action Plan on Social Exclusion*, London: Cabinet Office.

Sheppard, M. (2009) 'High thresholds and prevention in children's services: the impact of mothers' coping strategies on outcome of child and parenting problems – six month follow-up', *British Journal of Social Work*, vol 39, no 1.

Sibley, D. (1995) *Geographies of Exclusion*, London: Routledge.

SJPG (Social Justice Policy Group) (2006) *Breakdown Britain: Interim Report on the State of the Nation*, London: SJPG.

SJPG (Social Justice Policy Group) (2007a) *Breakdown Britain: Ending the Costs of Social Breakdown, vol 3 Educational Failure, Policy Recommendations to the Conservative Party*, London: SJPG.

SJPG (Social Justice Policy Group) (2007b) *Breakdown Britain: Ending the Costs of Social Breakdown, vol 6 Third Sector , Policy Recommendations to the Conservative Party*, London: SJPG.

SJPG (Social Justice Policy Group) (2007c) *Breakdown Britain: Ending the Costs of Social Breakdown, Policy Recommendations to the Conservative Party*, London: SJPG.

SJPG (Social Justice Policy Group) (2007d) *Breakdown Britain: Ending the Costs of Social Breakdown, vol 1 Family Breakdown, Policy Recommendations to the Conservative Party*, London: SJPG.

Sloper, P. (2004) 'Facilitators and barriers for co-ordinated multi-agency services', *Child: Care, Health and Development*, vol 30, no 6, pp 571-80.

Smith, R. (2003) *Youth Justice: Ideas, Policy, Practice*, Cullompton: Willan Publishing.

Social Exclusion Task Force (2007) *Reaching Out: Think Family*, London: Cabinet Office.

Social Exclusion Task Force (2008) *Think Family: Improving the Life Chances of Families at Risk*, London: Cabinet Office.

Thoburn, J., Chand, A. and Procter, J. (2004) *Child Welfare Services for Minority Ethnic Families: The Research Reviewed*, London: Jessica Kingsley Publishers.

Tilley, N. (2005) *Handbook of Crime Prevention and Community Safety*, Cullompton: Willan Publishing.

Tisdall, K. (2006) 'Antisocial behaviour legislation meets children's services: challenging perspectives on children, parents and the state', *Critical Social Policy*, vol 26, no 1, pp 101-20.

Townsend, P. (1997) 'Redistribution: the strategic alternative to privatisation', in A. Walker and C. Walker (eds) *Britain Divided: The Growth of Social Exclusion in the 1980s and 1990s*, London: Child Poverty Action Group.

Tunstill, J. (1997) 'Family support clauses of the 1989 Children Act', in N. Parton (ed) *Child Protection and Family Support: Tensions, Contradictions and Possibilities*, London: Routledge.

UNHCR (United Nations High Commissioner for Refugees) (2002) *Refugees, Asylum-Seekers and Other Persons of Concern: Trends in Displacement, Protection and Solutions*, Statistical Yearbook 2001, Geneva: UNHCR

UNICEF (United Nations Children's Fund) (2007) *Child Poverty in Perspective: An Overview of Child Well-Being in Rich Countries*, Report Card 7, Florence: UNICEF Innocenti Research Centre.

Van Cleemput, P. (2000) 'Health care needs of Travellers', *Archives of Disease in Childhood*, vol 82, no 1, pp 32-7.

Veit-Wilson, J. (1998) *Setting Adequacy Standards*, Bristol: The Policy Press.

Walters, R. (2007) 'Punishing "poor parents": "Respect", "Responsibility" and Parenting Orders in Scotland', *Youth Justice*, vol 7, no 1, pp 5-20.

Ward, N.J. (2005) 'Social exclusion and mental wellbeing: lesbian experiences', PhD thesis, University of Birmingham.

Warren, S. and Gillborn, D. (2003) *Race Equality and Education in Birmingham*, Birmingham: Equalities Division, Birmingham City Council and Birmingham Race Action Partnership.

Watson, D., Townsley, R., Abbott, D. and Latham, P. (2002) *Working Together? Multi-agency Working in Services to Disabled Children with Complex Health Care Needs and their Families: A Literature Review*, Birmingham: Handsel Trust.

Welshman, J. (2008) 'The cycle of deprivation: myths and misconceptions', *Children & Society*, vol 22, no 2, pp 75-85.

West, D.J. and Farrington, D. (1977) *The Delinquent Way of Life*, London: Heinemann.

Wikeley, F., Bullock, K., Muschamp, Y. and Ridge, T. (2007) *Educational Relationships Outside School: Why Access is Important*, York: JRF.

Williams, F. (2004) *Rethinking Families*, London: Calouste Gulbenkian Foundation.

Wintour, P. (2006) 'New taskforce to focus on alleviation of social exclusion', *The Guardian*, www.guardian.co.uk/politics/2006/jun/13/uk.socialexclusion

Wood, M. (2005) *The Victimisation of Young People: Findings from the Crime and Justice Survey 2003: Home Office Findings 246*, London: Home Office.

Woodhead, D. (2000) *The Health and Well-Being of Asylum Seekers and Refugees*, London: King's Fund.

YJB (Youth Justice Board) (2005) *Risk and Protective Factors*, London: YJB.

Index